WORLD TALES

The extraordinary coincidence of stories told in all times, in all places

ISBN 978-1-78479-231-2

First published 1979
Published in this edition 2015

Requests for permission to reprint, reproduce etc., to:
The Permissions Department
ISF Publishing
The Idries Shah Foundation
P. O. Box 71911
London NW2 9QA
United Kingdom
permissions@isf-publishing.org

In association with The Idries Shah Foundation

The ISF Collectors' Library

Tales of A Parrot and Other Stories

The Happiest Man in The World
and Other Stories

The Food of Paradise
and Other Stories

The Water of Life and Other Stories

The Land Where Time Stood Still
and Other Stories

This special edition of *World Tales*
is limited to five hundred copies.

Of which this is number 196.

The Water of Life and Other Stories

VOLUME IV

Collected by
IDRIES SHAH

The ISF Collectors' Library

'That lurking air of hidden meanings and immemorial mythical signs which we find in some fables, recalling a people, wise and childish at once, who had built up a theory of the world ages before Aesop was born.'
— Ernest Rhys, 1925

'The content of folklore is metaphysics. Our inability to see this is due primarily to our abysmal ignorance of metaphysics and its technical terms.'
— A. K. Coomaraswamy

'The folktale is the primer of the picture-language of the soul.'
— Joseph Campbell

'They (tales) appeal to our rational and irrational instincts, to our visions and dreams... The race is richer in human and cultural values for its splendid heritage of old magic tales.'
— Dr Leonard W. Roberts

Introduction

It is quite usual to find collections of tales arranged according to language or country: *Tales of Belgium*, *Stories from the German*, or *Legends from the Indian Peoples*; some such titles must have met your eye at one time or another. It all looks very tidy, scientific even; and the study of stories is indeed a part of scholarly research.

But the deeper you go into things, the more mysterious, exciting, baffling they become. How can it be that the same story is found in Scotland and also in pre-Columbian America? Was the story of Aladdin and his Wonderful Lamp really taken from Wales (where it has been found) to the ancient East; and, if so, by whom and when? A classical Japanese narrative is part of the gypsy repertoire in Europe; where shall we pigeonhole it in national terms?

I have selected and place before you a collection of tales of which one at least goes back to the ancient Egyptian of several thousand years ago. It is presented here not to impress the reader with its age, but because it is entertaining, and also because, although the Pharaohs died out many centuries ago, this tale is recited by people all over the world who know nothing of its origins. This form of culture remains when nations, languages and faiths have long since died.

There is an almost uncanny persistence and

durability in the tale which cannot be accounted for in the present state of knowledge. Not only does it constantly appear in different incarnations which can be mapped – as the Tar-Baby story carried from Africa to America, and medieval Arabian stories from the Saracens in Sicily to the Italy of today – but from time to time remarkable collections are assembled and enjoy a phenomenal vogue: after which they lapse and are reborn, perhaps in another culture, perhaps centuries later: to delight, attract, thrill, captivate yet another audience.

Such was the great *Panchatantra*, the Far Eastern collection of tales for the education of Indian princes; the Jataka Buddhist birth-stories believed to date back two and a half thousand years; the *Thousand and One Nights*, known as 'The Mother of Tales'. Later came the collections of Straparola, Boccaccio, Chaucer and Shakespeare, and a dozen others which now form the very basis of the classical literature of Europe and Asia.

This book contains stories from all of these collections, and many more: because there is a certain basic fund of human fictions which recur, again and again, and never seem to lose their compelling attraction. Many traditional tales have a surface meaning (perhaps just a socially uplifting one) and a secondary, inner significance, which is rarely glimpsed consciously, but which nevertheless acts powerfully upon our minds. Tales have always been used, so far as we can judge, for spiritual as well as social purposes: and as parables with more or less obvious meanings this use is familiar to most people today. But, as Professor Geoffrey Parrinder says of the myth, 'its inner truth was realised when the participant was transported into the realm of the sacred and eternal.'*

Perhaps above all the tale fulfils the function not of escape but of hope. The suspending of ordinary constraints helps people to reclaim optimism and to fuel the imagination with energy for the attainment of goals: whether moral or material. Maxim Gorky realised this when he wrote: 'In tales people fly through the air on a magic carpet, walk in seven-league boots, build castles overnight; the tales opened up for me a new world where some free and all-fearless power reigned and inspired in me a dream of a better life.'

When relatively recent collectors of tales, such as Hans Christian Andersen, the Brothers Grimm, Perrault and others made their selections, they both re-established certain powerful tales in our cultures and left out others from the very vast riches of the world reservoir of stories. Paradoxically, by their very success in imprinting Cinderella, Puss-in-Boots and Beauty and the Beast anew for the modern reader (they are all very ancient tales, widely dispersed) they directed attention away from some of the most wonderful and arresting stories which did not feature

* G. Parrinder, Foreword to *Pears Encyclopaedia of Myths and Legends*, London 1976, p.10.

in their collections. Many of these stories are re-presented here.

Working for thirty-five years among the written and oral sources of our world heritage in tales, one feels a truly living element in them which is startlingly evident when one isolates the 'basic' stories: the ones which tend to have travelled farthest, to have featured in the largest number of classical collections, to have inspired great writers of the past and present.

One becomes aware, by this contact with the fund of tradition which constantly cries out to be projected anew, that the story in some elusive way is the basic form and inspiration. Thought or style, characterisation and belief, didactic and nationality, all recede to give place to the tale which feels almost as if it is demanding to be reborn through one's efforts. And yet those efforts themselves, in some strange way, are experienced as no more than the relatively poor expertise of the humblest midwife. It is the tale itself, when it emerges, which is king.

Erskine Caldwell, no less, has felt a similar power in the story, and is well aware of its primacy over mere thought of philosophy: 'A writer,' he says (*Atlantic Monthly*, July 1958) 'is not a great mind, he's not a great thinker, he's not a great philosopher, he's a story-teller.'

Idries Shah

Note: This is the full introduction as it appeared in the original version of *World Tales*

Contents

The Kindly Ghost

The Biblical story of 'Joseph and His Brothers' appearing as an African folktale, surprised some collectors. But the Sudan, where this example was collected by Amina Shah, is geographically and historically linked with Egypt, and the diffusion problem is not great, though it is not known how long this tale has been extant in oral form.

Much more puzzling is the appearance of this story in Hawaii (as 'Aukele and the Water of Life') and in at least one other version as well. This tale was recited to amazed missionaries by Polynesians before they had been told the Biblical versions. This narrative and other recognisably related tales from the world stock of stories are found among the Maoris of New Zealand, and in Tonga, the Marquesas and Samoa. They are, in fact, pan-Polynesian, and the themes involved are encountered, too, in cultures ranging from Zulu to Eskimo to Semitic.

Once there were three brothers, who were wandering about looking for water.

After a lot of walking, they got to where one tree was standing alone, far away from any other. They were very thirsty and tired, so they sat down under the tree. Presently, when they felt better, the two elder brothers said to each other, 'Let us go on further, and leave Ahmad here, as he will only be troublesome to us, for he cannot walk as fast as we can. And, if we do find water, why should we have to have one third each instead of half?'

So, when the younger brother slept, they both ran off and left him.

At last it was evening, the sun had gone down, and Ahmad woke with a start. 'Where are you, brothers?' he cried in fear, in the darkness. But there was no reply. He was terrified, and called again.

Suddenly a ripe fruit fell out of the tree and hit him on the shoulder. He ate it greedily, as it tasted delicious, and he thought he would not save any for his brothers. Wild animals began to call in the surrounding desert land, so Ahmad quickly got into the hollow of the tree. It was comfortable and safe from the prowling creatures that hunted at night. When his eyes were accustomed to the dark, he saw that he was in a little room inside the tree, and there was a fine bow lying at his feet with a set of hunting arrows beside it. There was also an axe, made of sharpest steel. In the morning, after he had had a good sleep, he went out with the axe, cut bark and creepers from the tree, and made a snare for animals. Hunting far and wide, he shot game. When he was thirsty the tree seemed to know, and dropped a sweet juicy fruit from its topmost branches.

Time went by – he did not know how long – but day after day he managed to feed himself, and to quench his thirst from the fruit of the tree. In all that time there was no rain.

He was happy, though he kept wondering when his brothers would be returning. He never gave up hope that they would come back to find him when they discovered where there was water.

One day, he found there was a small rat in his snare. He bent over it and heard it squeak: 'Let me out, let me out, and when you need me, I will repay your kindness.'

He was very surprised to hear the rat speak with a human voice. He released it, and it darted away.

The next day, when he came back from hunting, he found he had trapped a falcon. 'If you will let me free, I shall repay your kindness just when you need it,' said the bird, in a human voice.

Ahmad released it, and it flew away high into the sky, without saying any more.

When night came, he squeezed himself into the hollow of the tree, and inside he saw the vision of a small grey man. 'How are you, my son? Have you got everything you need?' he asked, kindly.

'Not everything, father,' said Ahmad, 'but sufficient for each day and night, I thank you.'

The old man said, 'Once upon a time, in the distant past, I, too, lived in this tree, and I was so skilled in magical things that I only wished for a thing for it to immediately appear before me. But of what use is anyone's poor magical power in the World of Worlds?'

Ahmad looked on in amazement, hearing the old man talk, and seeing how radiant he appeared in the darkness of the tree's hollow. He could not speak for wonder. 'This will be of use to you,' went on the old man. 'It is a magical pouch, and if you wish for something, it will make that thing happen. But wish for no evil thing, or evil will come upon you. Take your rest now, and when you need something, wish upon my magic pouch.'

The vision vanished, and Ahmad scarcely knew whether he had imagined him or not, except that the magic pouch was in his own hand.

When morning came he rose, and went out into the dawn and looked around. All was desolate as before. With the magic pouch clasped in his fingers, he wished with all his heart for a village to spring up there, and trees, water and friendly people. No sooner had he wished than there was a great rushing sound in his ears. He closed his eyes, and when he opened them, there was so much activity around him he was nearly pushed over. There were people buying and selling under his tree, there were goats bleating, small boys running and shouting, women carrying huge bundles hither and thither on their heads. There were several huts nearby, and old men were sitting outside them, smoking. Best of all, there flowed nearby a fine, sparkling river.

Ahmad ran to the water and, throwing himself down, splashed cold water on his face. He was in Paradise, he thought. Now, walking around, with the magic pouch tied to his belt, he found it was a real village, though it also appeared to be the village of his dreams.

A respectable-looking elder beckoned him over to his doorway. 'Ahmad, welcome to your very own village,' said he. 'Go, take those cattle over there; they are yours.' And he pointed to a large herd of the finest animals Ahmad had ever seen.

The days passed with many delights, and soon he was married to a pretty wife.

One night, the little old ghost appeared to him and Ahmad said to him, 'Thank you so much for all the wonderful things I have got through the miraculous pouch.'

'Do not thank me,' said the old man, 'I am not the One who has wrought these things.'

'Well, take the pouch back, then, and give it to

whomsoever it belongs,' said Ahmad.

'No, my son, you will still have need of it, it is yours for life,' said the ghostly visitor, and vanished.

One evening, just as the sun had set, Ahmad and his wife were looking out towards the river, when they saw two dusty, dirty, dishevelled men staggering towards the village. They were none other than Ahmad's two brothers.

'Brother, brother!' cried the elder, throwing himself at Ahmad's feet, 'let us stay here and rest. We have searched so long for water, and now we have been told that you own this village and this river, and all these cattle. Please forgive us for leaving you, take us in and let us stay for a little while!'

Ahmad raised them up, and gave them clean clothes, food and shelter. He asked them to stay in his village, and be with him and his wife for as long as they wished.

But instead of being really grateful, the two brothers began to be jealous of all that Ahmad now owned, and the respect which he was given by the villagers. One night they came to him and said, 'O brother, we are nothing here compared to you; we are going away.'

And Ahmad clenched his hands over the magic pouch and said, 'Let my brothers have each as fine a house as I have, and pretty wives, and cattle, and let them be content.' New houses sprang up, more cattle appeared, and two pretty wives came to the two men.

The brothers were amazed at the magical properties of the pouch which was hanging from Ahmad's belt, and asked, 'Is that the source of all your wealth?' and Ahmad told them, 'Yes, it was given to me in a dream by a little old man, and it is by holding it and wishing, that I have got everything I have today.'

Then the brothers said, 'Let us have a look at that fabulous pouch, then, so that we can see for ourselves,' and Ahmad handed it over.

No sooner had the elder brother got the pouch in his grasp than he cried, 'Let this village and all that is in it be swept away to a faraway place, and this part become desert again, with our dear brother Ahmad wandering about in it!'

No sooner were the words out of his mouth than the village, the river, the cattle and the people completely disappeared. Ahmad once more found himself alone, without anything to his name but a ragged shirt and broken sandals.

He could not understand what had happened. Surely it could not be due to his two brothers' greed and jealousy?

'Please, old grey father, tell me what to do!' he cried in vain. No voice answered him, no kindly old man appeared.

Far away, far from where Ahmad was lamenting,

the happy people of his village laughed and played no more. They went about the day's work sadly, and with averted faces. The wicked brothers lived like despotic monarchs, forcing everyone to bow down to them.

Ahmad's pretty young wife sat alone in her house, eating nothing, grieving for her husband. What had happened, she did not know, except that without him she wanted to die, as Ahmad seemed to have deserted her.

But, now something else happened. Each night, the two brothers got no peace at all, for the ghost of the old grey man went from one to the other, singing and moaning, and wailing, giving out strange sounds all night long. They got up in the morning weary and fretful, and dared not go to bed for fear of the old ghost. No matter where they slept, they could not escape him.

All this time Ahmad was wandering and looking for his village and his wife, when one day a rat jumped out of a hole in the ground at his feet. 'Ahmad, good Ahmad, listen to me... You allowed me to escape when I was caught in your snare, I will help you now. You are apparently in trouble, with no bow or arrows, no food in your belly, so far from water. What is the matter?'

Ahmad told the rat the whole story from beginning to end.

'Good deeds are not often repaid by kindness,' said the rat, 'bitter indeed is ingratitude. But wait, I will get the magic pouch back for you.' And he darted away.

Ahmad sat down beside the rat's hole and waited. After all, he had nothing to lose by waiting, the sun was not yet overhead, and he needed to rest, anyway.

The two brothers were fighting at that moment as to who was the true owner of the pouch. As it went from one to the other, it fell on the ground. In came the rat and snatched it between his teeth. 'Stop that rat, it's taking away the magic bag!' cried the elder brother. The second brother picked it up, with the rat still clinging to it. They beat the rat with sticks, but still it held on. Then, from the sky swooped a falcon, the one which Ahmad had released, and took the pouch in its beak. The rat escaped and ran away.

Soon the pouch was laid at Ahmad's feet by the falcon. As soon as the pouch was in his fingers Ahmad wished that his village could be returned to him with all it contained. No sooner were the words out of his mouth than he heard the lowing of his cattle, and his pretty wife came towards him, with laughing eyes. But the two false brothers came to Ahmad with false smiles on their faces, and pretended that they knew nothing about the matter of the village being spirited away.

Ahmad looked at them, and saw them for what they were. He knew that if they remained there, trouble would always be in the air.

'Their ways are not my ways,' said Ahmad to the

magic pouch, 'please let them be taken away to a village of their own where I will never go, and may I never set eyes upon them again!'

The two brothers vanished before his very eyes.

So, ever afterwards, the rat played in Ahmad's hut, and the falcon flew over the roof, and the magic pouch hung in readiness at his waist.

The Ass in Pantherskin

While such fables as the Fox and the Grapes and the Wolf in Sheep's Clothing have become proverbial in many countries, this one is important in the literary history of 'Aesopian' teachings. It originates with The Panchatantra *('The Five Books'), dating at the latest from 500 AD, and perhaps as old as 100 BC. It was compiled for the instruction in government of princes in India. It is one of the most widely translated books in the world; there are over two hundred versions in more than fifty languages.*

This particular fable is of interest because it is one of the only two stories from The Panchatantra *which are attributed to Aesop (the other is 'The Ass without Heart and Ears'), and also because it is found in the works of Lucian and the Fables attributed to Babrius (third century AD) and also in the Fables of Avian.*

*Professor Franklin Edgerton of Yale University (*The Panchatantra*; London: Allen & Unwin, 1965) has pointed out that part of the original zest of the story is the fact that, in*

India, the ass is considered the epitome of lecherousness.

'The Five Books' is a very worldly primer, preaching mainly that one should look out for oneself. This may not have been so true of the original work which seems to have foreshadowed it. The translations, starting from the 6th century AD. Pahlavi Iranian version, are from a lost Sanskrit original. There is a persistent belief in the Middle East and West Asia that the versions which we have are superficial in having been adapted from spiritual into political teaching. One interpretation of the following tale, for instance, along these lines, states that the skin covering the ass stands for hypocrisy or the assumption of mystical knowledge, which are thrown off when the real nature of the human being (the braying) breaks through under stress.

THERE WAS ONCE a donkey belonging to a washerman, which was exhausted through carrying heavy loads of laundry. His owner, to help him recover, put a panther's skin over him for warmth and turned him into someone else's field to graze.

The ass could eat as much as it liked, for people thought that he was a panther and did not drive him off, and so he revived somewhat.

A certain farmer, glimpsing the wild animal's skin, was greatly afraid and stole away as cautiously as he might, wrapped in his grey cloak.

But the donkey, seeing what he took for a female ass in the distance, started to run after it. The man put on speed. The ass thought that he would give a mating-call, in case his quarry had mistaken him for a panther.

As soon as the man heard the donkey braying, he knew what he was, and, drawing his bow, killed him on the spot.

The Water of Life

The idea of the Water of Life is very widespread in European traditional lore and in the East. This tale from the Grimm collection resembles one from The Thousand and One Nights. *This version of the story was shown, over a hundred and fifty years after being published in Germany from a narrative of the countryfolk of Hesse, to a Yemenite bard. This interesting experiment showed that the illiterate reciter of tales claimed instantly to recognise it as a metaphor of the spiritual search and its perils. He interpreted the 'water' as mystical understanding, the 'father' as the community, the 'bad brothers' as spurious religionists, and much more. Story-tellers like this Taimur Rasuli draw great crowds in the Middle East, and have repertoires of some hundreds of tales and variants.*

Once upon a time, many many years ago, in a far distant land, there was a King who had three sons. One day, this King became ill and nobody knew how to cure him.

His sons were very sad about this, and one day, as they were walking in the gardens of the palace, wondering what to do, they suddenly saw an old man who came up to them and asked them what the matter was. When they told him, the old man said: 'There is something that will cure your father. It is the Water of Life. All he needs is one drink of it, but it is very difficult to find.'

Now the eldest son said to himself: 'If I manage to find the Water of Life for my father, he is sure to appoint me as the next King.' In that country the King always appointed his own successor.

At first the King said: 'No, I have heard that the search for the Water of Life is dangerous, and I would not have you do such a thing.' But the young man insisted, and finally the father gave him permission to go.

So the Prince set out on horseback. After journeying for some time, he came to a very deep valley with rocks all around him, and he saw a little man with a strange hat and cloak. And the little man said:

'Where are you going, Prince?'

The Prince said: 'That's nothing to you, you insolent fellow,' and he rode his horse impatiently past the little man.

Now the little man thought that this Prince was being discourteous and through his special powers he made it impossible for the Prince to move any further. The Prince found that he couldn't go forward, he couldn't go back, he couldn't get off the horse. In fact, he couldn't do anything, and all he heard was laughter all round him.

Now, in the meantime, the old King was waiting and waiting, and so were the brothers, for the return of the eldest Prince. And when they got no news, the second son said: 'Father, I shall now go and bring back the Water of Life.'

At first the King did not want to let him go, but in the end he gave his permission, and the second son set out. As he went on his way this Prince said to himself: 'I shall bring back the Water of Life to cure my father and he will surely make me his heir.'

Now, the Prince, as he went along the road, met the same little man who stopped his brother. And the little man said: 'Prince, where are you off to?'

The Prince, who was very rude, said: 'Be off with you! I have no time for you.' And he rode scornfully past. The little man put the same spell on this Prince as he had put on his eldest brother; and he, too, found himself paralysed and unable to move.

Now, when the second Prince didn't come back when the old King and the youngest son had waited and waited for news, the youngest Prince went to his father and said: 'Father, I will now go and bring the Water of Life for you.' At first the father did not want him to go, but finally he reluctantly agreed.

So the young man set off, and when he got to the same spot where his brother had met the little man, he saw him sitting there, with his funny hat and cloak. The little man said to him: 'Where are you going, Prince?'

And the Prince said: 'I am going to find the Water of Life to cure my father. Can you help me?'

And the little old man said: 'Do you know anything about how or where to find the Water of Life?'

'No,' said the Prince.

'Well,' said the little man, 'since you have been courteous to me and you are intelligent enough to know that you need advice, I will tell you. The Water of Life is found in a well, in a magic castle. Now I will give you a wand of iron and two loaves of bread. When you get to the castle, strike its door of iron three times with the rod, and it will open. Inside you will find two hungry lions. Throw down the loaves, and you will be able to pass them safely. Then, hurry on to the well inside and take some of the Water of Life before the bell strikes. But if you stay there too long, the door of iron will close – and you will never be able to escape.'

The Prince thanked the little man and took the rod and the bread and went on, and on, over sea and over land, until he came to the end of his journey. And he found everything as the little man had said. When the door had flown open, and when the lions were eating the bread, he saw he had come into a huge, enormous hall. In the hall there were a number of people sitting around, as if in a trance. And he took rings off their hands and put them on his fingers; and in another room there was a table with a sword and a loaf of bread on it, which he also collected.

Then he came to a room where there was a beautiful maiden sitting on a couch, and she welcomed him and said: 'Set me free, and you may have my kingdom. If you come back in a year and a day the magic spell will have worn out, and we shall be able to get married.'

He said: 'I must go and get the Water of Life for my father who is ailing, but I shall return in a year and a day.'

And the Princess said: 'Very well, go through that door and you will find the Water of Life.'

He went through the door, and saw a well in the inner gardens of the castle, and he took some water and put it into a bottle.

Now the youngest Prince felt that his mission was all but accomplished; and when he saw a beautiful couch with silken draperies on it, he thought he would just sit down and rest.

He sat down, but he soon fell asleep. Then,

suddenly he woke, hearing a sort of rattle, which was the bell starting to strike. So he jumped up from the couch and, taking up the bottle of water, the loaf and the sword, he managed to get out of the iron door just before it closed.

Then the young Prince started to journey homeward, and his way led through a country where everybody was starving. He gave them some of the bread which he had taken from the table in the magic castle, and they found that there was magic bread enough for everybody in the whole country. But the Prince did not have time to receive their thanks. He spurred his horse on; and then he came to a country which was dreadfully threatened by a terrible enemy. So he handed the sword from the castle to the King of that country, because it was a magic sword which would defeat any enemy. Then the young man urged his horse on, and finally he came to the little man who had told him where to look for the Water of Life. He said to the little man: 'I am in a great hurry to get back to my father, but I wonder what happened to my two brothers who set off in front of me to find the Water of Life?'

The little man said: 'They were so insolent, they were so arrogant, and they valued advice and knowledge so little, that I have paralysed them with a spell.'

The young Prince asked that they should be released, and the little man said: 'Very well then, I shall release them for your sake, but I warn you, they are very bad people and no good will come of this.'

'They are my brothers, however,' said the youngest Prince. And so, eventually, the little man let them go.

The three princes now set off for their father's bedside. And, as they went, the youngest Prince told his brothers the whole story of his adventures.

But when the young man was asleep one night on the homeward journey, the two brothers plotted his downfall. They stole the Water of Life and put some ordinary water instead into the bottle in which he carried it. And so, when all three arrived back at their father's Court, the elder brothers had the real Water of Life.

The young Prince went forward and gave his water to his father, and since it was only ordinary water the old King was not made any better at all. Then the two other Princes produced their water, saying: 'Here, father, is the *real* Water of Life. Our brother is not telling the truth. He never found the real Water of Life. *We* had the adventures which he claims to have been his.'

The old King sipped the water; and as he did, he was completely and at once restored to health. He became so angry at what he thought was the deceitfulness of his youngest son that he sent him away with a soldier to be killed, and then he rewarded his two other sons with costly gifts.

Now the young Prince was led into the forest by the soldier, and the soldier seemed rather sad. So the young Prince said to him: 'My friend, I have been unjustly accused. I am quite innocent of the charges laid against me.'

The soldier said: 'I am afraid it is my duty to kill you.'

But the young Prince said: 'Give me your cloak and I will give you mine. You can take my cloak back to the King and say that you have killed me. And I promise to disappear for ever.'

The soldier agreed, and the young man plunged into the forest. Now, it was not long afterwards that a resplendent embassy arrived from the country which had been saved from famine by the young Prince, with the full story of how it had been he, and no one else, who had saved their country. And then, not long afterwards, rich gifts were sent from the second kingdom, which had been saved by the young man through the magic sword.

Now, the old King realised that his two elder sons had not been telling the truth. And he said, 'It is very sad that I had him put to death without giving adequate thought to the matter.'

And the soldier, as it happened, was present in Court when the King said this aloud. And he stepped forward and said: 'Your Majesty, he is still alive. I took pity on him, although I did disobey your orders.' And he explained what had happened.

The King was overjoyed and sent messages to all the Kings and Princes of the world, explaining that he had unjustly accused his son and that he wanted him to come home again.

Meanwhile the Princess in the enchanted castle was eagerly awaiting the return of the youngest Prince. She had a road of gold made leading from the palace some distance to the main highway. And she gave orders that whoever came straight up the golden road and did not follow it to the right or left, would be her lover. And anybody else would not be the true youngest Prince and should be taken into custody.

The young Prince, meanwhile, was making his way as well as he could, to try to fulfil his promise to rescue the Princess in a year and a day.

Now the two other brothers, knowing the story of the Princess in the magic castle, and fearing the wrath of their father, decided to go and try to capture her for themselves. They got on their horses, and they rode far and they rode fast.

When they got to the golden road, one said: 'This road is too beautiful to ride on,' and he turned his horse and rode on the right-hand side of it. The guards, when they saw him do this, took him immediately in charge.

And the second Prince, when he saw the golden road thought: 'This road is too beautiful, I must not tread on it,' and he, too, turned; and he rode on its left side. And the guards, when they saw this, imprisoned him.

Eventually, travelling slowly, the young Prince arrived at the golden road. And when he got to its edge he just glimpsed the castle and he thought only of the Princess and could see no other form of beauty. The road was completely invisible to him, because he thought only of being reunited with his beloved. He went straight down the middle of the road, up to the iron gates. And the guards let him in.

The Princess was overjoyed at his arrival and after they had embraced one another, she told him that she had received a message from his father the King, saying that all was now well. The young Prince told her the whole story of the treachery of his brothers, and the Princess said: 'They are here, my guards are holding them in the dungeons.'

So the young Prince said: 'Let them go.'

And as soon as they were released, they fled by ship to some very remote place, and have never been seen since.

So the young man and the Princess went to celebrate their wedding at the court of the old King. And they invited everybody, including the first old man and the little old man who had advised them so well.

And everyone lived happily ever after.

The Serpent

The animal fable has long been one of the most favoured formats for preaching and the inculcation of morals in both East and West. In the East, notably India, while animals are generally shown to be good rather than bad, fables are often employed to warn against giving trust or making assumptions where certain kinds of people – symbolised by animals – are concerned.

The fable of the serpent was for centuries one of the most popular and most widely used. In the Middle Ages, it did service to Christianity, through the Clerical Discipline *of the baptised Jew Petrus Alfonsus of 800 years ago, in the monkish* Gesta Romanorum *of the 13th century, and John of Capua's* Directorium Humanae Vitae. *Before that, it served Islam in the Persian* Fables of Bidpai*; and even earlier it is found counselling Hindus in the pages of an anecdote of King Vikramaditya of Ujjain and elsewhere. The story has been found extant and still flourishing in popular narrative in both Italy and the Himalayan region of Asia. Choosing a version which is geographically in between, we can look at the Balkan one, collected in Albania*

THERE WAS ONCE a hunter who, while passing by a quarry, noticed that a serpent was trapped by a large stone or rock.

The snake called out when it saw him: 'Please help me, lift the stone.'

The hunter answered: 'I cannot help you, because you are likely to devour me.'

The reptile asked again for aid, promising that he would not eat the man.

And so the man released the snake. It immediately made a movement towards him, as if to attack.

'Did you not promise not to eat me, if I let you go?' the man asked.

The snake said: 'Hunger is hunger.'

'But,' said the hunter, 'if you are doing something wrong, what has hunger to do with it?'

The man then suggested that they should put the matter to the adjudication of others.

They went into some woods, where they found a hound. They asked him whether he thought that the snake should eat the man, and he replied:

'I was once owned by a man. I caught hares, and he would provide me with the very best meat to eat. But now I am old, and I cannot even catch a tortoise, so he wants to kill me. Since I have only been given evil in return for good, this is what the snake should give to you. I claim that he should eat you.'

'You have heard,' said the snake to the man. 'That

is the judgement.'

But they decided to take three pieces of advice, not one, and continued on their way. Presently they met a horse and asked him to judge between them.

'I think that the serpent should be allowed to eat the man,' said the horse. It continued:

'I once had a master. He fed me for so long as I could travel. Now that I am feeble and cannot continue my duties, he desires to kill me.'

The serpent said to the man: 'We now have the unanimity of two judgements.'

Further along, they came across a fox. The hunter said:

'Dear friend, come to my help! I was passing a quarry and I found this huge serpent under a stone and almost dead. He asked me to release him. I got him out, and yet he now wishes to eat me.'

The fox answered:

'If I have to give a decision, let us return to the place where you met. I have to see the actual situation.'

They went back to the quarry, and the fox asked for the rock to be placed over the serpent, to reconstruct the situation. This was done. He asked: 'Is this how it was?'

'Yes,' said the serpent.

'Very well,' the fox told him. 'You shall now stay there until the end of your days.'

The Wonderful Lamp

Ordinary readers have always associated the tale of Aladdin and the Wonderful Lamp with the Arabian Nights. *Scholars, who could not find it in any version known to them, accused the French translator Galland of making it up himself and passing it off as an Eastern story. They were far too hasty. It has, since the 18th century, been found in Oriental manuscripts of South India and Burma and in Albania. It exists in the oral literature of the Mongolians, in Greek and in Czech. Ms M. H. Burke took the following oral version from the lips of an almost illiterate woman in Rome, where it may have been current for centuries.*

ONE DAY A kindly-looking old man knocked at the door of a poor tailor's house. His small son opened the door, and the visitor said that he was his uncle, and gave the lad a coin to buy himself a meal. Now the tailor, who was out of work, was away at the time, but later he came home, and was rather surprised to find his guest calling him his brother. Still, as he seemed to be rich, he did not feel inclined to object too strongly.

The newcomer spent some time with the family, spending liberally on their upkeep; but finally said that he had to leave, and wanted to take the boy, Cajusse, with him, so that he might learn something and so become a businessman. Of course the tailor agreed.

As soon as they had left the town, however, the man said, 'I am not really your uncle at all. I need a strong lad to perform a task which I am too old to complete. I am a magician. Now, don't try to get away – you cannot.'

Cajusse was not particularly alarmed, and asked the wizard what he had to do. The man took up a stone slab from the ground and told the boy that he had to go down into the earth. 'When you get to the bottom of the cave, continue along until you come to a beautiful garden, where you will find a fierce dog, keeping guard. Give him this bread. Do not, on any account, look back if you hear any noise behind you. You will see an ancient lamp on a shelf. Take it down and bring it back to me.'

Then the wizard gave Cajusse a ring. 'If anything happens,' he said, 'rub the ring and wish to be saved from it.'

Cajusse duly made his way underground, where he found all kinds of amazing things. Precious jewels hung like fruit from trees, and he picked many and filled his pockets with them. When he got back to the entrance of the cave, the old man asked him to hand up the lamp.

'Not until you have pulled me up,' said Cajusse, fearful that he might be left behind on his own.

The magician, to frighten Cajusse, dropped the stone slab back into the cave's entrance. But Cajusse simply rubbed his ring, and an apparition manifested itself. 'Bring food for supper!' cried Cajusse. He also ordered his parents to be brought to him, so they all had a wonderful meal.

Cajusse returned to his home. Some time later, he heard that the town was to be illuminated to celebrate the wedding of the Sultan's daughter to the son of the Chief Minister. He had an idea. 'Mother,' he said, 'I want to marry the Princess. Take this basket of priceless jewels to the Sultan, and say that we ask for his daughter in marriage.'

The old woman did as she was bid, and the Sultan was truly astonished when he saw that the jewels were more precious than anything which he had in his own treasury. He promised to give his answer at the end of a month.

It was so arranged, however, that the Princess and the Minister's son were married within the week. Cajusse rubbed the magic lamp and said, 'Tonight go and take away the daughter of the Sultan, and place her on a mattress of straw in our outhouse.'

When the Princess appeared on the palliasse, Cajusse placed a naked sword between them in token of the purity of his intentions, and lay beside her, wanting to talk. But the Princess – not unnaturally – was far too afraid of him to reply.

Cajusse had the Princess carried three times, one night after another, to his home; and the girl told her mother about it, unable to understand what was happening.

The Queen told the Sultan, and he was just as puzzled. And the Minister's son complained to his father that his bride kept disappearing when night fell, and returned in some inexplicable way, at dawn.

Cajusse sent his mother to the Sultan again, this time with three baskets of priceless gems, asking if he could be allowed to see the Princess. 'Very well,' said the Sultan, 'he may come to the Palace.'

As soon as he heard that he was to be received by the royal family, Cajusse rubbed his magical ring and caused magnificent robes of gold and silver to be brought, together with a beautiful horse and attendants, who walked ahead of him strewing money and crying: 'Make way for Signor Cajusse!'

The Princess obtained her liberty from the Minister's son, and she and Cajusse were married.

But the wizard, of course, heard about Cajusse's successes, and he decided to get hold of the magical lamp. Dressing himself as a pedlar, he stood outside Cajusse's house, calling out: 'Old lamps taken and new ones given for them!' Cajusse was not at home, and the Princess sent out the ancient lamp in the hands of a servant, which the magician exchanged for a new one. Then he rubbed the lamp and caused the palace to be borne away by magic to an island somewhere in the remote seas.

When Cajusse arrived home, he realised what had happened and rubbed his magical ring, which never left his finger, asking to be carried by the slave of the ring to where the palace was now located.

When he got there, Cajusse blew his horn outside the window of his wife, and she rushed to it, to assure him that she would refuse the magician's attempts to make her his wife. Cajusse advised her: 'Arrange a feast tonight. Tell the magician that you will marry him only if he will tell you what thing would be deadly for him, so that you can protect him against it.'

Sure enough, there was such a secret, and during the feast the wizard confided it to the lady. 'In a far away forest,' he said, 'there is a beast called a hydra, which has seven heads. Someone desiring my death would have to go there, find the animal and cut off his seven heads. When the middle head is split open, a young hare will leap forth and run away. If the hare's head is split open, a bird will fly out. If the bird is caught and split open, a precious stone will be found in his body. If that stone is placed under my pillow, I shall die.'

Now, of course, Cajusse knew what to do. He travelled to the forest, and found the hydra, which he killed. When he split its middle head, the hare jumped out. Cajusse caught the hare and cut its head open, out flew the bird. He managed to catch the bird and open it up. Inside was the stone, which Cajusse hastened to take to the Princess, together with a bottle of opium.

In the evening, the girl slipped some of the drug into the magician's wine, and he fell into a deep sleep. As soon as the stone was placed under his pillow, he uttered three terrible cries, turned around three times, and died.

Now that the awful sorcerer was dead, Cajusse and his wife, by means of their magical things, had the palace returned to where it had been before, and lived happily ever afterwards.

Who Was the Most Generous?

The kind of tale which was enjoyed in Europe about six hundred years ago is that of the freeholder (The Franklin) in Chaucer's The Canterbury Tales. *Like the Italian Boccaccio, whose hundred tales were published when Chaucer was a child, Chaucer incorporated this tale of effort and generosity plus romance into his stories. These were supposedly told by a group of people to each other to pass the time.*

The theme of the lady who is reluctant to yield to a suitor and who therefore sets him tests – which may or may not be successfully carried out – seems to have been of abiding interest to all kinds of writers and readers in the past. On this theme, numerous ancient Hindu story-tellers contrive to make the would-be lover ashamed; so do the Arabians. The Persians have the husband test his wife, and she turns the tables on him. In an English story of 1430 – 'The Lady Prioress and her Three Wooers' – the devout lady punishes a knight, a priest, and a merchant, who all have designs on her chastity. An unexpected twist occurs in the story of 'The Lady of Antwerp'; she sets tests for three lovers and herself dies in the end.

Chaucer's 'Franklin's Tale' covers much of the same ground, but it introduces the question of chivalry, and gives an insight into what must have been the way of thinking of those remote times, from the pen of the first writer of relatively modern English. It certainly is unusual to find the husband, the wife and the lover and his accomplice all tied for the accolade of generosity – and the moral left open for the reader.

ONCE THERE WAS a noble cavalier who loved a beautiful Lady. After he married her, another cavalier courted her secretly, which she abominated, but she dared not tell her husband of the intrigue, lest there be bloodshed.

Tarolfo, the second nobleman, troubled her so much by letters, flowers and small gifts of love, that the Lady told him she must see him. He arrived at a hidden bower, feeling that he must surely have won her.

But he was in for a surprise.

'My good sir,' said she, 'there is only one situation in which we can be lovers. When my garden shall bloom in cold January with the flowers of mild June.'

'I swear that I shall not rest until I have learned how this can be done, dear Lady,' said he, leaving with his head high.

'That shall never be,' said she, and went to her boudoir, secure in the belief that she would not see him again.

But Tarolfo went to Thessaly, where he chanced upon an ancient man, gathering herbs in a dark wood. 'What do you do, Sir?' he asked the old man, and the answer was 'I am collecting for physic. Who are you and what do you here?'

'I am from the farthest West, I grieve over a most hopeless position, yet I have still hope, for the prize is very great,' said Tarolfo.

The old man, who was called Tebano, said, 'I will

help you if you tell me what it is that you have to do.'

The cavalier told him, 'I must make a garden blossom in January with all the flowers of summer.'

'It can be done,' said the old man. 'Do you not know this is an uncanny place you have come to?'

'God will protect me,' said the nobleman.

'Do not judge me by my outside appearance. I can do anything that is required, if the payment is right. What will you give me if I perform this service for you?'

'You shall have half of whatever I own, half of my horses, half of my sheep, treasure and houses,' promised Tarolfo, so eager was he to gain the love of the Lady.

The magician agreed, and they went to the garden, in January, on the night of a full moon. With mystic movements and strange utterances, the old man cavorted around the garden. By dawn everything was in flower as if it were midsummer. Roses and fair blossoms were everywhere. 'By my faith', cried the Lady, upon rising, 'the garden is blooming with every flower of summer. I am undone!'

Soon a message came from her would-be lover, requesting that she give him a time when they could be together, as he had fulfilled her condition.

Nearly out of her mind with distress, she sent him a letter to say that she must wait until her husband was away from home.

Now, her husband, loving her much, noticed that

she neither smiled nor ate for the space of a week, and questioned her. 'Is it your health, my love, or your mind?' he asked anxiously. Unable to bear the shame, she told him everything, and waited for his condemnation. It did not come. Instead he said gravely, 'You made a promise, even though it was a rash one, but as you are bound by your word, you must keep it. You should go to him, but, my dear, do not in future make any promise such as this – even though it does seem impossible.'

'You mean I should let him enjoy me as he wishes?' she cried.

'Yes,' said he, 'Tarolfo has earned his reward. He has kept his word, now you must do so.'

With her maidens around her, she sadly went to meet the cavalier at the appointed place. All adorned she went, yet her heart was heavy and she dreaded his approach. 'Does your husband know?' was his first question.

'Yes, he sent me to you so that I should keep my word,' she replied.

Tarolfo thought for a moment, then he said:

'Please return to your husband. He is so generous a man that I cannot take what is rightfully his.' A look of shame came to his face. 'Beg him to forgive me, I will never do anything so ignoble as this again.'

She thanked him and returned to her husband, full of joy. Her lesson had been hard, but she had learned it.

Now, the magician, when Tarolfo went to him and said, ‘Come, take your half of my possessions,’ was not pleased.

‘I cannot take payment for what has not been a successful enterprise,’ he said, shaking his head. ‘I have a pride in my work. After all, am I not a craftsman just as any carpenter or builder is? The gods forbid that I should be less generous than the husband has been.’ And he disappeared before Tarolfo’s very eyes.

Now, which of the three was the most generous?

Cupid and Psyche

The strange fascination of legends in which people turn into animals – or the other way about – have given us both Beauty and the Beast and the Frog Prince. The forbidden, the taboo of looking or of knowing something before due time, is usually integral with the legend, found all over Europe and in Asia. Thomas H. Moore has collected a version from Chile. Sometimes, as in the Indian tales, the lady is an enchanted snake; in Norway the girl is married to a white bear; elsewhere, she may have a magical bird-costume which effects the transformation. Some scholars think that the whole idea is derived from ancient Egypt, and alludes to the metamorphosis of the Butterfly, Aurelia, and hence is a parable of the ascent of the human soul. One of the most distinguished versions of the legend is this one, from Apuleius' The Golden Ass, of the 2nd Century AD.

ONCE UPON A time there was a great King, who had three fair daughters. And they were so beautiful that from many lands suitors came to seek their hands in marriage.

The youngest was the loveliest of all, so that people said that she was like the goddess Aphrodite, and they bowed low as she passed through the streets of the city.

Now it was not long since Paris had given the goddess Aphrodite the apple for being the fairest of all the goddesses, and she was jealous. She summoned her son, Cupid, and said to him, 'Come, let us fly together to see this mortal maiden whom men say is the image of me.' They reached the palace where Psyche was sleeping, and when his mother showed the girl to him, she said to him: 'Prick her with one of the arrows of love so that she will feel the deepest affection for one of the basest of mortal men. Avenge me, my son.' Then she departed.

Cupid, however, gazing upon the girl, was stricken with pity and said, 'I will never do you so much wrong as to mate you with some wretch not good enough for you. You are safe from my darts.' And he flew away.

Now, though all men bowed down before Psyche, none dared marry her, for she seemed too good and pure. So while her sisters married, and had husbands whom they loved, Psyche remained untouched and unsought. When she had reached the age when Greek maidens should be wed, the King grew anxious, and went to consult the oracle. When he returned, with ashen face, his Queen asked him what had been the oracle's answer. 'Psyche must be left on a desolate mountainside until some monster comes to devour her,' said the King. 'Men have paid her honours only reserved for the gods, and the gods require vengeance.'

The Queen and her maidens wept and wailed, but Psyche remained calm. At last a white-clad priest came to tell the King he must tarry no longer. Soon a procession, each person clad in black, left the city, Psyche led by her father and mother, and singers sang a mournful dirge. The sun was rising when they reached a bare rock; and here it was that the oracle had directed Psyche should be left to perish.

When for the last time her parents took her in their arms, Psyche never shed a tear in farewell. After all, what good was it to mourn, when it was surely all the will of the gods?

Not daring to look back, in case they should see the dreadful monster actually devouring their daughter, the King and Queen went away with their retainers. Psyche was very tired, for she had walked a long way, so she leaned wearily against the rock. Soon a deep sleep came over her, and her sorrows were forgotten.

While she slept, Cupid was looking down at her, and at his bidding Zephyr lifted her up gently and carried her away to lay her down upon a bed of lilies in the valley.

While she slept, beautiful dreams wafted through her mind. She woke feeling happy, she did not know why, and, getting to her feet, began to walk towards a beautiful palace made of ivory and gold. A little timidly, she stepped into the palace, and passed from room to room without coming to the end of the wonders there. Out of the silence a voice said in her ear: 'Everything you see is yours, so enjoy the palace and its contents as if it were your own home.' There was a table set with every delicacy, forks and spoons of gold, and unseen fingers played music upon the harp.

When evening came, a great calm came upon Psyche, and she heard someone say, 'Place this veil upon your head, for you are to be a bride,' and a golden veil descended upon her, covering her face. Then a cake was put into her hand, and the same voice said, 'Eat half of this cake and I will eat the other half.' She did so with trembling fingers, and she saw that the rest of the cake had vanished. 'Now listen to what I say,' she heard the voice again. 'You are now my wife, and you will live in this palace with me as long as you live. But, one word of warning: your sisters may find you here, and if they come, do not tell them anything about this ceremony, for their love can turn to hate very quickly, out of jealousy.'

Psyche nodded, and promised that she would do as her unseen husband decreed. But after a few weeks of bliss she began to feel unhappy at being without friends of her own age, and sometimes cried beside the fountain. One evening she felt her husband's fingers stroking her hair, asking, 'What makes you so unhappy, my dear?'

'It is because I miss my sisters and my friends,' she answered, and continued, 'Could I not see my sisters even for a little while? After all, I have not been devoured by any monster, they might like to know what has happened to me.'

There was silence for a few moments; then the voice said, 'I am afraid that ill may come of your wish, but if you remember what I told you and do not tell them everything, I am happy for you to invite your sisters here.' Psyche was overjoyed, and promised to tell them nothing.

'Then, tomorrow,' said he, 'I shall tell my servant, Zephyr, to carry them here.'

And next morning Zephyr found her sisters seated on the rock, beating their breasts and crying. Suddenly, they found themselves wafted gently to the palace where Psyche was sitting. Soon they were laughing together, and the great table was groaning with food and silver, and they ate till they could eat no more.

'Now, tell us what happened to you after you were left on that dreadful rock,' asked the eldest sister; and the other enquired, 'Where is your husband?

and *who* is he?'

Their growing suspicion boded no good for Psyche, and she began to be afraid for her secret. 'Oh, he goes out hunting a lot,' she said. 'I would like you to come into the treasure-room with me and choose some presents.'

The sight of so much gold and so many jewels and precious objects turned their heads completely. The gifts they were given were of immense value, and when Zephyr bore the girls away, unknown to them, Psyche felt that she did not want to see her sisters again for quite some time.

'You told them nothing, I hope?' asked her husband that night. 'For they could be plotting your downfall, you know…'

'No, I remembered what you said, husband, and indeed I was glad to see them go, for they have become very jealous of me,' said Psyche.

'Good,' said he, sighing, 'for the present moment all seems well, but be careful that you do not let them know the true state of affairs, or much ill fortune will come to us.'

'I promise you,' said Psyche, 'I will never tell them. Let them come again, and I will show you how I can be silent!'

So the sisters came again, Psyche wanting to show her husband that he could trust her completely.

At first the other two girls behaved as if they were

glad of their sister's good fortune, then one said, 'Oh, dearest sister, I've been so worried about you and the dreadful thing which had happened to you that I can scarcely speak.'

'Why, what do you mean?' asked Psyche, trembling. Her blood ran cold when she saw the look on their faces. 'Tell me, and do not beat about the bush. What is it?'

'Your husband, dear sister, who is he? Where is he from? From where does he get all this treasure? My dear, believe us, we are only thinking of your own good…' and the two sisters began to wring their hands.

Psyche shook her elder sister's arm and said: 'Tell me, what have you heard about my husband?'

'We have it on the very best authority,' said her sister, 'that your husband is not as you think, but a huge and poisonous snake which is full of venom. People working in the fields have seen it swimming across the river. Believe us, we would not like to tell you this, but…'

Psyche recoiled with horror. 'It is true I have never yet seen my husband's face,' she cried. 'He warned me that if ever I were to look upon him he would be forced to abandon me forever. And yet, and yet, he is always so gentle to me.'

'We have something here to help you see his true form,' the sisters chorused, placing a small oil-lamp into Psyche's hand. 'Tonight, when he is asleep, light this and look upon that dreadful face. Then you can happily return with us and be free of him!'

They both embraced her, and were wafted home on the wings of Zephyr.

Left alone, Psyche wept, and for hours tried to subdue her misery. When at last her husband came in, she managed to hide her deceit. So well did she feign happiness that he did not suspect anything was wrong as she welcomed him. Soon he was asleep by her side. For a few moments Psyche wondered whether she dare light the lamp or not, then she felt she had to know. She leaned over the bed and held the flame close to him. Instead of the dreadful monster she had expected there was the most beautiful of all the gods, Cupid himself.

At this sight Psyche started and a drop of burning oil fell on Cupid's shoulder. He woke, and looked at her reproachfully. He turned, and would have flown away, but Psyche grasped his leg, and was borne up with him into the air, till she fell to the ground and fainted away.

Then, after she had regained consciousness, she spent a long time searching and calling for her husband, weeping and begging him to return. Wandering through the country, one day she came to a temple, where she saw sheaves of oats, ears of corn and scythes all scattered in wild confusion. Attempting to bring some order to the chaos, she began to tidy the place; and then she heard a loud voice from afar: 'Unhappy girl! You have brought down the wrath of the goddess Aphrodite on your head. Go, leave this temple in case you also draw down on me the fury of the goddess.'

Not knowing where her feet would lead her, Psyche wandered on, still searching and crying. At last she was tracked down by one of Aphrodite's servants, who took her to the sacred presence of the goddess herself. Here she was whipped and beaten, and was made to separate a large heap of seeds of all kinds – wheat, millet, barley. The task seemed to be hopeless, but Aphrodite left her to do it, under strict instructions from the goddess to put each of them in an individual pile. As she sat and wept, a tiny ant came, and seeing her plight, brought all his brothers, and by nightfall every grain was sorted and in its own bag. Psyche waited, trembling with fear, for Aphrodite to enter the room.

When she did enter, Aphrodite was seized with anger and cried: 'Wretched girl! It is not through your own labour that this has been done! Now, in yonder glade, there are some sheep whose coats are as bright as gold and as soft as silk. Tomorrow morning at dawn I want you to go out there, shear them, and bring in enough wool to make me a robe. And this time I do not think you will have any help!' So saying, she disappeared.

Next day, very early, Psyche went out to the glade, and looked into the clear waters of the river. A reed sang to her: 'O Psyche, fear nothing. The sheep must be shorn at evening, for during the day you will not be able to catch them. When they lie exhausted, you can gather all the wool you need from the branches of the shrubs and the hedges through which they have been rushing wildly all day.'

So Psyche did as the reed told her, and waited till the cool of the evening, and gathered enough wool for the goddess. But when she gave it to Aphrodite, she was greeted with scowls of rage and ordered to go to the top of a lofty mountain to fill an urn from a fountain of black water. The urn was of the finest crystal, and Psyche carried it up most carefully in case she should drop it. But when she got there she found the fountain was guarded by two terrible dragons. She would have started back without the water, had not a giant eagle taken the vessel from her hand and filled it, telling the dragons that Aphrodite needed the precious water to add fresh lustre to her beauty.

Joyfully the eagle brought Psyche the precious urn filled with the black water, and she gave it to the goddess. But still Aphrodite was not satisfied. Each time she was given new tasks and errands, birds and beasts helped her, and the goddess was quite frustrated in her desire to destroy Psyche.

If Cupid had only known that Psyche was

suffering so many privations, he would have somehow contrived to save her, but the wound where the boiling oil had fallen took a long time to heal. At last, when it was completely healed, he visited Psyche, and she was overjoyed at the sound of his voice. She poured out all the story of her sufferings, and Cupid was grieved for her. He said, 'Your punishment has been more than a mortal ought to be asked to endure, and though I am not able to save you from my mother's wrath, I will fly to Mount Olympus, and beseech the gods to grant you forgiveness.'

And so he did. In the fullness of time Psyche was rescued from her trials on Earth, and left the world of humans, to sit among the immortals on Mount Olympus, forever immortal herself.

The Royal Detectives

The historian Herodotus, in the fourth century BC, recorded this tale from, as he says, ancient Egyptian priests: a narrative which has been called the first detective story. Yet it is one of the world's most widely distributed folktales, and is known to the people of Scotland and Mongolia, Norway and Tibet, Cyprus and Russia, as well as in France, Germany, Greece, Armenia, Wales and North Africa. It is very widely dispersed among the world's gypsies, in the Master-Thief versions. One scholar believes that the Gypsy telling is the original one, even more complete than the ancient Egyptian. It is believed to have entered European literature in the 12th century, in the Latin 'Seven Wise Masters'. Many versions claim or imply that they are historical fact, and supply names and places where the events are said to have happened. Six hundred years ago the place given is the palace of the Doge of Venice and the thief is named Bindo; in Denmark, the robber is Klaus and the treasury that of Count Geert of Jutland. For the French, the crime took place at Morlaix, the Russian name of the robber is Chibarca, and in Holland he is from Bruges.

THE EGYPTIAN KING Rhampsinitus had a great abundance of silver, at that time rarer and more valuable than gold. He ordered a certain builder to make a treasure-house abutting upon the wall of the palace.

Now this builder, when he was about to die, called his two sons to him and told them that he had placed one of the stone blocks on pivots so that even one man could move it, and thus enter the chamber from outside. In this way the sons would be able to steal as much of the King's wealth as they wished.

As soon as their father was dead, these two young men went to the palace wall at night, found the stone and entered the treasure-room. They took away a considerable quantity of the treasure.

The King could not understand what had happened to his silver, when he entered the room whose seals were unbroken and saw how much was missing. So he set a trap after the third opening of the room.

One of the lads was caught in this trap, and could not move. He at once asked his brother to cut off his head and carry it away, so that he could not be recognised and bring trouble upon the whole family.

This the brother did, leaving the treasury by the same secret way in which he had entered it.

The King was astonished to see the headless body, and wondered how he could track down the thieves. He decided to have the trunk hung on the palace's outside wall under guard. The guards were to arrest and bring to the King anyone seen weeping or making a commotion before the body.

The dead thief's mother, when she came to know that the body of her son was suspended in this way, was greatly disturbed. She asked the surviving son to do anything he could to get the body back. If he did not obey her, she said, she would go to the King and confess.

So the youth took some donkeys and loaded them with skins full of wine. He drove them past the guards and made sure that some of the skins fell to the ground, while he pretended to be occupied with the donkeys. The guards stole some of the wine-skins, thinking themselves very clever.

Then the thief acted as if he was very angry with the guards, but they spoke kindly to him, and he appeared to be mollified. He got his asses into proper order again, and then became so friendly with the guards that he gave them some more of his wine. They all began to drink, and they consumed one wineskinful after another until the guards were befuddled and lay down to sleep.

In the dead of night the thief stepped over the sleeping guards and took his brother's body away on his donkeys.

The King, when he heard of this exploit, was

naturally furious, and was even more determined than ever to locate the thief. He told his daughter to receive and to make friends with anyone from the city who came to her, and to challenge him to tell her the greatest trick and crime he could think of. If anyone told her the story of the headless thief, she should seize hold of his hand and cry out so that he could be arrested.

The thief, however, heard of the plan, and went to the girl with a dead man's arm concealed under his robe. He told her that his greatest crime had been to rob the King's treasure in the way already described, and that his greatest trick had been to fool the palace guards as he had done.

When the Princess seized the arm which he held out, he stole away in the darkness, leaving her with the severed limb.

When the King heard of this, he announced that if the thief would declare himself, he would be rewarded. The thief revealed himself, and the King gave him his daughter as a reward for his cleverness.

Conflict of the Magicians

The 'Magical Conflict' theme is found in the Arabian Nights *and Germany (in the collection of the Grimms), in Mongolia and Norway, in Gaelic, Danish, Welsh, Italian and many other languages. People as diverse as the Albanians of East Europe, the Tamils of South India, the Austrians and the Kalmucks have thrilled to its incidents, which have few variations, for longer than any recorded literature can tell. The story given here is from the great Kalmuck collection, the* Siddhi Kur, *translated by Professor Jülg. The teacher Nagarguna referred to at the end of the story died in 212 BC. This and other supposedly Buddhist legends are found in the great Welsh traditional collection,* The Mabinogion. *In this version, the story is given as an account of Taliesin, the Welsh bard of the 6th century. Found in the Library of Jesus College, Oxford, it is the distinguished translation of Lady Charlotte Guest, believed to be the earliest European version.*

In the Kingdom of Magadha there once lived seven brothers, and the strange thing about them was that they were all magicians: they could do all kinds of amazing things, and nobody knew how they carried out their enchantments.

A mile or so from where they lived was the house of two brothers who were the sons of a Khan, a local ruler. The elder of these two wanted to learn magic; so he went to the seven magicians, and he said:

'Teach me to understand your art,' and he stayed with them for seven years, trying to find out their secrets.

But the magicians kept him very busy, doing all kinds of tasks, and they never taught him the key to their mystic knowledge.

One day, however, the younger brother came to visit him and, looking through a crack in the door into the room where the magicians were at work, managed to learn and to understand the whole of their magical science.

And so the two sons of the Khan went home together: the elder because he could never learn anything from the magicians and the younger because he had learnt everything that they knew.

As they went along, the younger brother said:

'Now that I have obtained all their secrets, the seven magicians will probably want to do us some harm. So you go to the stable – which we left empty.

There you will now find a wonderful horse. Put a bridle on him, and lead him out to sell. Make sure that you do not go in the direction of the magicians. When you have sold him, bring back the money you have received.'

When he had said this, he went away, turned himself into a horse with the spells he had learnt, and entered the stable to wait for his brother to collect him for sale.

But the elder brother, since the magicians had told him nothing, was not afraid of them at all. He said to himself:

'If my brother is so clever that he can conjure a fine horse into the stable, let him produce another one for us to sell: I'll keep this one for myself.'

So he saddled and bridled the horse; but he found that he could not control him. Because he was not taking him to sell, and having forgotten to avoid the magicians' house, he soon found that the animal had borne him away and was standing by the door of the house of the warlocks.

The elder brother now decided that the best thing to do would be to sell the horse, and he offered it to the magicians at a high price. They realised that it was magical, and they said to one another:

'We must prevent the spread of magical horses and things of that kind; otherwise they will become too common, and people will not come to us to buy our wonders. Let us get this horse and kill it.'

The magicians paid the asking price, took the horse which was really the enchanted younger brother, and shut it up in a dark stall. When they were ready to slaughter it, one of them held it by the tail, another by the head, and the others by its legs, so that it could not break away.

When the young man who had become a horse realised what they were about to do, seeing the knife in the hand of the seventh magician, he thought:

'I wish that any other living being could appear, so that I might put myself into it!'

Hardly was this thought formed in his head than a little fish came swimming down a nearby stream, and the son of the Khan, in some strange way, went into it: he became the fish.

But the seven magician brothers knew what had happened, and they turned themselves into seven large fish, which followed the small one. When they were very close to the little fish, with their mouths wide open to swallow him, the son of the Khan said, within himself:

'I wish that any other living being could appear, so that I might put myself into it!'

All at once there was a dove, flying in the air, and the Khan's son became the dove. The seven magicians, seeing what had happened, transformed themselves into seven hawks, and pursued the dove over hills and dales, and nearly overtook him when it took refuge in Tibet.

There is a shining mountain southwards in Tibet, and the dove managed to enter a cave there, called the Giver of Rest. There the dove went into the presence of the Great Teacher Nagarguna.

The seven magicians, at the entrance to the cave, changed themselves into pious men, dressed in cotton garments.

They entered the presence of the Master, and humbly requested that he give them his rosary: because, by then, the dove had changed itself into a single bead on the string carried by the Great Teacher.

But Nagarguna understood inwardly what was happening. He handed them the chaplet: but not before he had taken off the single bead which was the dwelling of the son of the Khan. He dropped the bead out of his mouth: and it instantly became a man again, with a great and wonderful stick. Now the son of the Khan took the stick and slew the magicians who had been posing as pilgrims.

False Witnesses

This tale is thought to have been brought to the West by Jacques, Bishop of Acre, Palestine, who took part in the Crusades and died in Rome in 1240 AD. Its message – that people will often accept the assertions of the majority however contrary to the evidence of their own senses – has been verified in the 20th century by psychologists. The earliest English version is that of 1518, and it is found in Hebrew, Persian, German, Spanish, Syriac and Latin as well. The essential idea, however, has been traced back nearly fifteen centuries, but it may have been first composed more than 2000 years ago. This version is from the 15th-century German adventures of the Saxon rogue Till Eulenspiegel, called in English 'Howelglass' or 'Owlglass'.

THE CUNNING OWLGLASS went to a fair where all kinds of things were being sold, to see what he could get for nothing. He laid his plans to see whether he could trap a peasant. After looking around for a time, he espied a countryman buying a nice piece of green cloth. 'This,' he decided, 'will do for me, I shall get hold of the cloth...'

'Good morning,' he said to the farmer, 'and where did you buy that fine bolt of blue cloth?'

'It isn't blue, it is green.'

'What nonsense,' said Owlglass, 'you must be blind: anyone can see that it is the deepest and surest blue.'

The argument went on, with the peasant getting more and more annoyed, until they decided that the first person to come along should be asked to judge the colour. 'What is more,' said the peasant, 'if this cloth is blue, then I'll forfeit it, and you can have it yourself, for nothing!'

Now Owlglass had a friend, a rogue priest, with whom he had already arranged the trick. At a signal, the priest came out of where he was hiding, looking like the first passer-by.

'Hey, there!' shouted the villain, 'Sir Priest, will you pronounce upon the colour of this cloth, to settle an argument?'

'Indeed I will my son,' said the priest, 'it is undoubtedly blue, as anyone can see.'

'Now give me the cloth, you ignorant oaf!' cried Owlglass.

'Not likely' – the peasant was cunning – 'for how do I know that you have not arranged all this with the priest, to steal my cloth?'

'Very well,' said the crook, 'let us wait until the next man approaches.'

Sure enough, within a minute or two, another figure strode past, and was called in to judge. He, too, was a confederate of the first two confidence men – and he insisted that the cloth was blue.

So Owlglass won his wager, the cloth was handed over, and the three crooks divided the spoils.

The Cobbler Who Became an Astrologer

The theme of surprise: things turning out well when the opposite is expected, and the other way about, is today as well represented in detective and science fiction as it has been in world tales of the past. Whether it is the nagging wife or some other external cause, the principle in this kind of story is that someone is set on a course not of his – or her – own choosing. Beyond the exciting cause, however, there is the stream of destiny, which has its own plans, which themselves interlock with the fates of the other characters in the narrative. In this case there is an interplay among the lives of the cobbler, the jeweller, the Queen, the thieves, and so on, which seeks to indicate – so say traditional story-tellers – that people and events do not exist in isolation. Furthermore, the results of actions cannot be predicted only from expectation, however well-informed.

It is believed by some Oriental thinkers that tales such as this illustrate the workings of the extra-dimensional world which can sometimes be entered by those who have been prepared to handle its seeming confusion – by means of a tale such as this:

THERE WAS IN the city of Isfahan a poor cobbler called Ahmed, who was possessed of a singularly greedy and envious wife. Every day the woman went to the public baths, the Hammam, and each time saw someone there of whom she became jealous. One day she espied a lady dressed in a magnificent robe, jewels on every finger, pearls in her ears, and attended by many persons. Asking whom this might be, she was told, 'The wife of the King's chief astrologer.'

'Of course, that is what my wretched Ahmed must become, an astrologer,' thought the cobbler's wife, and rushed home as fast as her feet would carry her.

The cobbler, seeing her face, asked, 'What in the world is the matter, my dear one?'

'Don't you speak to me or come near me until you become a Court Astrologer!' she snapped. 'Give up your vile trade of mending shoes! I shall never be happy until we are rich!'

'Astrologer! Astrologer!' cried Ahmed, 'What qualifications have I to read the stars? You must be mad!'

'I neither know nor care how you do it, just become an astrologer by tomorrow or I will go back to my father's house and seek a divorce,' she said.

The cobbler was out of his mind with worry. How was he to become an astrologer? – that was the question. He could not bear the thought of losing his wife, so he went out and bought a table of the zodiac signs, an astrolabe and an astronomical almanac. To do this he had to sell his cobblers' tools, and so felt he must succeed as an astrologer. He went out into the market-place, crying, 'O people, come to me for all answers to everything! I can read the stars, I know the sun, the moon and the twelve signs of the zodiac! I can foretell that which is to happen!'

Now, it so happened that the King's jeweller was passing by, in great distress at losing one of the crown jewels which had been entrusted to him for polishing. This was a great ruby, and he had searched for it high and low without success.

The Court Jeweller knew that if he did not find it his head would be forfeit. He came up to the crowd surrounding Ahmed, and asked what was happening.

'Oh, the very latest astrologer, Ahmed the Cobbler, now promises to tell everything there is to know!' laughed one of the bystanders.

The Court Jeweller pressed forward and whispered into Ahmed's ear, 'If you understand your art, discover for me the King's ruby, and I will give you two hundred pieces of gold. If you do not succeed, I will be instrumental in bringing about your death!'

Ahmed was thunderstruck. He put a hand to his brow and shaking his head, thinking of his wife said: 'O woman, woman, you are more baneful to the happiness of man than the vilest serpent!'

Now, the jewel had been secreted by the jeweller's

wife, who, guilty about the theft, had sent a female slave to follow her husband everywhere. This slave, on hearing the new astrologer cry out about a woman who was as poisonous as a serpent, thought that all must be discovered, and ran back to the house to tell her mistress. 'You are found out, dear mistress,' she panted. 'You are discovered by a hateful astrologer! Go to him, lady, and plead with the wretch to be merciful, for if he tells your husband you are lost.'

The woman then threw on her veil, and went to Ahmed and flung herself at his feet, crying, 'Spare my honour and my life and I will tell all!'

'Tell what?' enquired Ahmed.

'Oh, nothing that you do not know already!' she wept. 'You know well I stole the ruby. I did so to punish my husband, he uses me so cruelly! But you, O most wonderful man from whom nothing is hidden, command me, and I will do whatever you ask that this secret never sees the light.'

Ahmed thought quickly, then said, 'I know all you have done, and to save you I ask you to do this: place the ruby at once under your husband's pillow, and forget all about it.'

The jeweller's wife returned home, and did as she was bidden. In an hour Ahmed followed her, and told the jeweller that he had made his calculations, and by the sun, moon and stars the ruby was at that moment lying under his pillow.

The jeweller ran from the room like a hunted stag, and returned a few moments later the happiest of men. He embraced Ahmed like a brother, and placed a bag containing two hundred pieces of gold at his feet.

The praises of the jeweller ringing in his ears, Ahmed returned home grateful that he could now satisfy his wife's lust for money. He thought he would have to work no more, but he was disenchanted to hear her say, 'This is only your first adventure in this new way of life! Once your name gets known, you will soon be summoned to court!'

Unhappily, Ahmed remonstrated with her. He had no wish to go further in this career of fortune-telling, it simply was not safe. How could he expect to have further strokes of luck like the last, he asked? But his wife burst into tears, and again threatened him with divorce.

Ahmed agreed to sally forth next day to the marketplace, to advertise himself once more.

He exclaimed loudly as before, 'I am an astrologer! I can see everything which will happen, by the power given to me by the sun, the moon and the stars!'

The crowd gathered again, and a veiled lady was passing, while Ahmed was holding forth. She paused with her maid, and heard of the success he had had the day before with the finding of the King's ruby, together with a dozen other stories which had never happened. The lady, very tall and dressed in fine silks, pushed her way forward and said, 'I ask you this conundrum: where are my necklace and earrings which I mislaid yesterday? I dare not tell my husband about the loss, as he is a very jealous man and may think I have given them to a lover. Do you, astrologer, tell me at once where they are, or I am dishonoured! If you give me the right answer, which should not be difficult for you, I will at once give you fifty pieces of gold.'

The unfortunate cobbler was speechless for a moment, on seeing such an important-looking lady before him, plucking at his arm, and he put a hand over his eyes. He looked at her again, wondering what he should say. Then he noticed that part of her face was showing, which was quite unsuitable for one of her social level, and the veil was torn, apparently in her pressing through the crowd. He leaned down and said in a quiet voice: 'Madam, look down to the rent, look to the rent!' He meant the rent in her veil, but it immediately touched off a recollection in her mind.

'Stay here, O Greatest of Astrologers,' she said, and returned home to her house, which was not far away. There, in the rent in her bathroom wall she discovered her necklace and earrings, where she herself had hidden them from prying eyes. Soon she was back, wearing another veil and carrying a bag containing fifty pieces of gold for Ahmed. The crowd pressed around him in wonder at this new example of the brilliance of the cobbler astrologer.

Ahmed's wife, however, could not yet rival the wife of the Chief Court Astrologer, so she still urged her husband to continue seeking fame and fortune.

Now, at this time, the King's treasury was robbed of forty chests of gold and jewels. Officers of state and the chief of police all tried to find the thieves but to no avail. At last, two servants were despatched to Ahmed to ask if he would solve the case of the missing chests.

The King's Astrologer, however, was spreading lies about Ahmed behind his back, and was heard to say that he gave Ahmed forty days to find the thieves, then, he prophesied, Ahmed would be hanged for not being able to do so.

Ahmed was summoned to the presence of the King, and bowed low before the sovereign.

'Who is the thief, then, according to the stars?' asked the King.

'It is very difficult yet to say, my calculations will take some time,' stammered Ahmed. 'But I will say this so far, Your Majesty, there was not one thief, but forty who did this dreadful robbery of Your Majesty's treasure.'

'Very well,' said the King. 'Where are they and what have they done with my gold and jewels?'

'I cannot say before forty days,' answered Ahmed, 'if Your Majesty will grant me that time to consult the stars. Each night, you see, there are different conjunctions to study…'

'I grant you forty days, then,' said the King. 'But, when they are past, if you do not have the answer, your life will be forfeit.'

The Court Astrologer looked very pleased, and smirked behind his beard, and that look made poor Ahmed very uncomfortable. Suppose the Court Astrologer was right after all? He returned to his home, and told his wife, 'My dear, I fear that your great greed has meant that I have now only forty more days to live. Let us cheerfully spend all we have made, for in that time I shall have to be executed.'

'But husband,' said she, 'you must find out the thieves in that time by the same method you found the King's ruby and the woman's necklace and earrings!'

'Foolish creature!' said he. 'Do you not recall that I found the answers to those two cases simply by the Will of Allah! I can never pull off such a trick again, not if I live to a hundred. No, I think the best thing will be for me each night to put a date in a bowl, and by the time there are forty in it, I shall know that is the night of the fortieth day, and the end of my life. You know I have no skill in reckoning, and shall never know if I do not do it this way.'

'Take courage,' said she, 'mean, spiritless wretch that you are, and think of something, even while we are putting the dates in the bowl, so that I may ever yet be attired like the wife of the Court Astrologer's wife, and placed in that rank of life to which my beauty has entitled me!' Not a word of kindness did she give him, not a thought for the turmoil that was in his heart, she only thought of herself and her personal victory over the wife of the Court Astrologer.

Meanwhile, the forty thieves, a few miles away from the city, had received accurate information regarding the measures taken to detect them. They were told by spies that the King had sent for Ahmed, and hearing that the cobbler had told of their exact number, feared for their lives. But the captain of the gang said, 'Let us go tonight, after dark, and listen outside his house, for in fact he might have made an inspired guess, and we might be worrying over nothing.'

Everybody approved of this scheme, so after nightfall one of the thieves listening on the terrace just after the cobbler had offered his evening prayer, heard Ahmed say, 'Ah, there is the first of the forty!' He had just been handed the first date by his wife. The thief, hearing these words, hurried back in consternation to the gang and told them that somehow, through wall and window, Ahmed had sensed his unseen presence and said, 'Ah, there is the *first* of the *forty*!'

The tale of the spy was not believed, and the next night two members of the band were sent to listen, completely hidden by darkness, outside the house. To their dismay they both heard Ahmed say quite distinctly: 'My dear wife, tonight there are two of them!' Ahmed, of course, having finished his evening prayer, had been given the second date by his wife.

The astonished thieves fled into the night, and told their companions what they had heard.

The next night three men were sent, and the fourth night four, and so for many nights they came just as Ahmed was putting the date into the bowl. On the last night they all went, and Ahmed cried loudly, 'Ah, the number is complete! Tonight the whole forty are here!'

All doubts were now removed. It was impossible that they could have been seen, under cover of darkness they had come, mingling with passers-by, and people of the town. Ahmed had never looked out of the window; had he done so, he would not even have been able to see them, so deeply were they hidden in the shadows.

'Let us bribe the cobbler-astrologer!' said the chief of the thieves. 'We will offer him as much of the booty as he wants, and then we will prevent him telling the chief of police about us tomorrow,' he whispered to the others.

They knocked at Ahmed's door; it was almost dawn.

Supposing it to be the soldiers coming to take him away to be executed, Ahmed came to the door in good spirits. He and his wife had spent half of the money on good living, and he was feeling quite ready to go. He did not even feel sorry that he was to leave his wife behind. She, in fact, was secretly pleased at having quite a lot of money left over to spend solely on herself.

'I know what you have come for!' he shouted out, as the cock crowed and the sun began to rise. 'Have patience, I am coming out to you now. But, what a wicked deed you are about to do!' and he stepped forward bravely.

'Most wonderful man,' cried the head of the thieves, 'we are fully convinced that you know why we have come, but can we not tempt you with two thousand pieces of gold and beg you to say nothing about the matter!'

'Say nothing about it?' said Ahmed. 'Do you honestly think it possible that I should suffer such gross wrong and injustice without making it known to all the world?'

'Have mercy upon us,' exclaimed the thieves, and most of them threw themselves at his feet. 'Only spare our lives and we shall return the treasure we stole!'

The cobbler was not sure if he were indeed awake or perhaps still sleeping, but, realising that these were the forty thieves, he assumed a solemn tone and said, 'Wretched men! You cannot escape from my penetration, which reaches to the sun and the moon, and knows every star in the sky. Your repentance has saved you. If you will restore every chest of the forty I will do my very best to intercede with the King on your behalf. But go now, get the treasure and place it in a ditch a foot deep which you must dig under the wall of the Old Hammam, the public baths. If you do this before the people of the city of Isfahan are up and about, your lives will be spared. If not, you shall all hang! Go, or destruction will fall upon you and your families!'

Stumbling and falling and picking themselves up, the band of thieves rushed away.

Would it work? Ahmed knew he only had a short time to wait and find out. It was a very long shot, but he knew that he had only one life to lose, and that he was in great danger anyway.

But Allah is just. Rewards suitable to their merits awaited Ahmed and his wife.

At midday Ahmed stood cheerfully before the King, who said, 'Your looks are promising, have you good news?'

'Your Majesty,' said Ahmed, 'the stars will only grant one or the other – the forty thieves or the forty chests of treasure. Will Your Majesty choose?'

'I should be sorry not to punish the thieves,' said the King, 'but if it must be so, I choose the treasure.'

'And you give the thieves a full and free pardon, O King?'

'I do,' said the monarch. 'Provided I find my treasure untouched.'

'Then follow me,' said Ahmed, and set off to the

Old Hammam.

The King and all his courtiers followed Ahmed, who most of the time was casting his eyes to Heaven and murmuring things under his breath, describing circles in the air the while.

When his prayer was finished, he pointed to the southern wall, and requested that His Majesty ask the slaves to dig, saying that the treasure would be found intact. In his heart of hearts he hoped it were true.

Within a short while all the forty chests were discovered, with all the royal seals intact.

The King's joy knew no bounds. He embraced Ahmed like a father, and immediately appointed him Chief Court Astrologer. 'I declare that you shall marry my only daughter,' he cried delightedly, 'as you have restored the fortunes of my kingdom, and to thus promote you is nothing less than my duty!'

The beautiful Princess, who was as lovely as the moon on her fourteenth night, was not dissatisfied with her father's choice, for she had seen Ahmed from afar and secretly loved him from the first glance.

The wheel of fortune had taken a complete turn. At dawn Ahmed was conversing with the band of thieves, bargaining with them; at dusk he was lord of a rich palace and the possessor of a fair, young, high-born wife who adored him. But this did not change his character, and he was as contented as a prince as he had been as a poor cobbler. His former wife, for whom he now had ceased to care, moved out of his life, and got the punishment to which her unreasonableness and unfeeling vanity had condemned her. Thus is the tapestry which is our life completed by the Great Designer.

The Two Travellers

The moral and magical tale of 'The Two Travellers' is found in a twelve-hundred-year-old Chinese book: and also in Norway, Africa, North America and Siberia. Its incidents are almost always very closely similar.

There are two men, one is treacherously blinded by the other. Deserted, he finds out (usually supernaturally) how to cure both himself and someone else who is in trouble. He does this and is rewarded: and then, in his honesty, tells the villain how he came about his fortune. The evildoer tries to copy his formula, but something dreadful happens to him instead.

In some versions (the African and one Gypsy telling) it is a bird or birds that save him. But, as often happens in traditional tales, the figure intervening changes according to cultural taste. In the Kirghiz form, it is a tiger, a fox and a wolf. In the Norse – where no tigers are to be found – the animals become a wolf, a fox and a hare. In the Thousand and One Nights *we find demons, as also in Bengal – and a spirit turns up again in Portugal. In south India, the secret knowledge comes from the goddess Kali, ordinarily a tutelary of destruction; but the Persian narrative softens the figure into that of a poor shepherd with special insights.*

In addition to folk versions, the story has a formidable literary pedigree. In Tibet, it is in the Kanjur, *in India it figures in* The Panchatantra*; in Iran the classical Nizami embodied it into his* Seven Portraits *of 1197. The Hebrew* Midrash Haggadol, *of about the 14th century, also has the story. Balkan Gypsy versions are known; and it was so popular in Russia that Afanasief's important collection contains no fewer than seven variants of the plot. This account embodies the usual common features of the tale.*

THERE WERE ONCE two men, one good and one bad, who went on a journey together. They were in quest of their fortune. The good man shared his food with his companion until it was all finished.

The good man then asked: 'May I have some of your food?'

'Certainly not,' said the other, and he became so irrationally infuriated that he plucked out the eyes of his unfortunate partner, robbed him of everything he had, and left him alone and helpless in the wilderness.

The blinded good man became aware of some birds singing, and decided to climb, feeling his way, into the tree in whose topmost branches they were, to be safe from any prowling wild beasts, at least until the morning, when he might be able to think of some way of continuing his journey.

Now it so happened that he found that he could understand the language of the birds. As he listened, he learnt from their discussions that any blind person who bathed his eyes in the dew of that place would have his sight restored. Further, the birds said that the daughter of a certain King was ill, but could be healed by the use of a flower which grew nearby. The same flower had the power of locating water and restoring fertility to gardens.

The blind man immediately bathed his eyes in the dew and found that he could see. Then he plucked the plant. He made his way to the place where the

Princess was ill and, having gained admittance, cured her. When he made the King's garden flourish again and found water which was badly needed, he was rewarded by being given the hand of the Princess in marriage.

He continued happily in this life, until the villain who had blinded him turned up again, having heard of his inexplicable good fortune. The miscreant asked him how he had arrived at such a happy and prosperous state.

'It was quite simple, in fact,' said the honest man, for he was one who bore no ill-will. 'All I did was go up a certain tree, and I heard what to do from the birds, whose speech I suddenly understood.'

The bad man thereupon hurried to the place where he had blinded his companion, and waited. Presently the birds arrived and perched on the top of the tree. He found that he understood their speech. They said:

'Someone has overheard our conversation, for the King's daughter is now well, the garden is blossoming, and water has been found!'

They looked all around to see whether an eavesdropper was about, saw the bad man, flew down – and pecked out his eyes.

The Fisherman and his Wife

Maxim Gorky, no victim of the sensation that world tales were merely irrationalities produced by disordered primitive brains, freely admitted that such stories 'opened up for me a new world where some free and all-fearless power reigned and inspired me to a dream of a better life'.

This tale certainly emphasises that there is another 'world' or system which can cause changes in this dimension which are utterly inexplicable. It also claims, implicitly, that there are rules connected with such phenomena which have to be observed.

In the oldest form of this recital, the Tibetan tale of King Mandhatar, the ruler conquers the whole earth and then desires to overwhelm heaven. Soon afterwards, he dies. A Polynesian connection has been noted, and there are many versions in Europe. Although the vanity and ambition of the King changes, in European hands, into that of a covetous woman, it might be noted that a check of folktale content has shown that more delinquent men than women appear in them, as a matter of statistics: and the sex of the culprit does not matter when it comes to the moral.

The following version gives a good idea of the climate and projection of the story in Germany of the time of the Grimm collection, with terminology somewhat modernised.

THERE WAS ONCE upon a time a fisherman and his wife, Isabel, who lived together in a little hut near the sea.

Every day he went down to fish, and sat with his rod for many an hour at a time, looking out upon the blank water.

One day, the line went right down to the bottom, and when he drew it up a great flounder was on the hook.

The flounder said: 'Fisherman, let me go, for I am not a real fish. I am an enchanted fish. What good will it do if you pull me up? I shall not taste good. Throw me back; you will soon catch another fish.'

'Ah,' said the fisherman, 'don't worry – as you can speak, you are obviously no ordinary fish. I will set you free.' So saying, he threw the fish back into the water. It swam away, leaving a streak of blood behind it.

Then the fisherman got up, and went back to his wife to tell her the strange happening.

No sooner did he get inside the hut than she said to him, 'Have you caught nothing today, husband?'

'Oh,' said he, 'I caught the most amazing fish. It could speak. It said that it was an enchanted fish, so I threw it back.'

'Did you do what you should have done, asked the fish for a wish first?' she asked.

'No,' said he. 'Why do you say that, wife?'

'Ah,' said she, 'that is very unlucky. Is one to remain in this hut forever? You might have asked for a better place in which we could live, at least. Go again, and call him, and say we need a better house. I'm sure out of gratitude he'll give it to you.'

'But how can that be managed?' he enquired.

'Well, catch him again, and before you release him, ask him quickly.'

The man was not very pleased, but his wife insisted, so more to get away from her than to catch the fish he went back to the sea. It looked grey and green, cold and uninviting. He stood by it and said:

'FLOUNDER, FLOUNDER IN THE SEA,
HITHER QUICKLY COME TO ME!
FOR MY WIFE, DEAR ISABEL,
WISHES WHAT I DARE NOT TELL.'

No sooner had he said this, than the Flounder came swimming up, and asked, 'What do you want with me?'

The man said, shamefacedly, 'My wife said I was to catch you again, and when I turned you loose I was to ask you if we could have a nice house instead of the hut.'

'Go home,' said the Flounder. 'You will be pleased.'

So the fisherman went home, and found instead of the hut, a clean cottage, with a white-painted gate. His wife was standing in the doorway, and said to him: 'Look, this is more like it. See the fine curtains, and the brass bed, the bright shiny copper pots.'

In the garden was a large apple tree, hens, chickens,

plenty of flowers and vegetables.

'Are you content?' asked the fisherman when they went to bed that night.

'I shall have to think about that,' said the wife, sleepily.

About fourteen days passed, and the fisherman caught enough for them each day. But his wife began to complain about the cottage, saying, 'Husband, the bed is too narrow, the parlour is too crowded, the kitchen much too small. The garden is draughty, the gate squeaks. Go then to the Flounder, and ask him for a castle for us.'

'Wife,' said he, exceedingly annoyed, 'I cannot do that again. Surely, this cottage is good enough for us.'

'Good enough for you, but not for me, I can tell you!' she replied angrily. 'Have you no ambition? Do you want to be a poor benighted fisherman living in a cottage like this all your life? Go, tell him what I have said.'

'It isn't right,' said the husband, 'I don't suppose I will ever see the Flounder again,' but he went down to the sea and looked out. The sea was quite choppy, with great waves topped by white crests. It looked green and grey no longer, but dangerous. 'The Flounder may be quite angry,' he thought, 'but I'd better try, just to tell Isabel that I did so.'

'FLOUNDER, FLOUNDER IN THE SEA,
HITHER QUICKLY COME TO ME!

FOR MY WIFE, DEAR ISABEL,
WISHES WHAT I SCARCE CAN TELL.'

'What do you want now?' asked the Flounder, swimming up with some difficulty.

'Oh,' said the man, half-frightened, 'she wants to live in a great big castle.'

'Go home,' said the Fish, 'she has it already.'

The fisherman went away, and could scarce believe his eyes. Where the cottage had been was a great stone castle, with turrets and battlements, slits for arrows and fifty stone steps. His wife called to him from the top of the stairs, and taking him by the hand, said, 'Now, let us walk about in our new home.'

So they walked about, in the great panelled hall, with tapestries hanging everywhere, and huge paintings of ancestors. There were gigantic oak tables, and silver, glass, linen; candelabras of Venetian work, rooms of treasure, many servants scurrying hither and thither. There were crystal looking-glasses, priceless carpets from the East, valuable hounds sitting beside the log fire. Outside there were stables, cow-sheds, dovecotes of gigantic size, waggons, flowers and fruit-trees. There were meadows full of deer, and oxen in the pasture, fat sheep in pens.

'Is this not charming?' said the wife.

'I hope you will be satisfied for life, with all this style,' said the bewildered fisherman, looking everywhere for his rod.

'We shall talk about that some other time,' said his wife.

All went well for about two or three weeks, then the wife said to her husband: 'Look from this window. Would it not be fine if you and I were King and Queen of all the land?'

'Woman, you must be mad!' said he. 'Have you not got enough?'

'Go,' she insisted, 'tell the Flounder we wish to be King and Queen.'

'I do not want to be King,' he shouted, 'I am a fisherman!'

'Be what you like,' she said. 'Just go and tell the Flounder that I want to be Queen. I *must* be Queen!'

He turned away and went down to the sea.

Stupefied, he looked out at the water. It was quite black, and when it splashed up it smelled most disagreeably. But he stood still and repeated as before:

'FLOUNDER, FLOUNDER IN THE SEA,
HITHER QUICKLY COME TO ME,
FOR MY WIFE, DEAR ISABEL,
WISHES WHAT I CANNOT TELL.'

'What does she want now?' asked the Flounder, swimming up with some difficulty.

'Ah,' said he, 'she wants to be Queen now.'

'Go home,' said the Flounder. 'She is Queen already.'

The man returned home, and when he came

nearer to his castle he saw it had become much larger, and that it had flags flying from the turrets, and soldiers on horseback standing guard everywhere. Before the gate was a herald, with a blaring trumpet, and there were other soldiers with kettledrums and fifes. When he went into the palace he saw there were items made of gold everywhere, plates and bowls set with precious gems. Magnificent curtains fringed with gold hung at all the windows. Tables were made of marble and gold, serious-looking courtiers strolled through the halls, deep in conversation.

He went into the great court apartments, and there sat his wife, with fountains playing jets of wine instead of water, upon a throne of gold and diamonds. She had a crown upon her head glittering with rubies and pearls, her hair in a net of gold. On her neck was a golden chain, in her hands a golden orb and sceptre. At each side stood six young pages, each dressed more gorgeously than the last.

The fisherman went up to his wife and said, 'Ah, Isabel, I see you are the Queen now.'

'Yes,' she said, 'I am Queen.'

'Do you like being Queen?' he asked. 'Now there is nothing else you can be.'

'Oh yes there is,' she snapped. 'Go to the Flounder right away and tell him that I must be, and shall be, Pope.'

'Oh wife, wife,' said he, 'you cannot be Pope: the

Pope is the head of Christendom and there is only one Pope. The Flounder cannot make you that!'

'I *will* be Pope,' said she, and he went off to find the Flounder.

When he came to the shore the sea was running extremely high, and the sky was so black he was quite terrified. The fisherman could hardly make himself heard above the sound of the mountainous waves which were breaking upon the rocks. He cried:

'FLOUNDER, FLOUNDER IN THE SEA,
QUICKLY, QUICKLY COME TO ME,
MY DEAR WIFE, QUEEN ISABEL,
WISHES WHAT I DARE NOT TELL.'

'What now?' asked the Flounder. 'She wants to be Pope,' said the man. 'Go home and find her so,' was the reply.

So he went back, and found a huge church, in which his wife was sitting upon a much higher throne than before, with two rows of candles on each side, and before her on footstools were Kings, Queens and Princes kneeling.

'Wife,' said he, 'be content. Since you are Pope, you can not be anything higher.'

'I will consider that,' she said haughtily, and turned her head away.

She rose very early next day, and looked out of the window, watching the sun rising.

'Why should I not make the sun rise and set?' she

asked herself. So she roused her poor husband, and said to him:

'I have thought of something. Go, tell the Flounder that I want to make the sun rise and set. Go quickly, I must be the Ruler of the Universe.'

Stumbling and falling, the fisherman made his way to the sea. There a tremendous storm was raging. Ships and boats of all shapes and sizes were tossing about in all directions. Then he shouted out, though the wind whipped his words away and he could not hear the sound of his own voice:

'FLOUNDER, FLOUNDER, IN THE SEA,
QUICKLY, QUICKLY, COME TO ME,
FOR MY WIFE, POPE ISABEL,
WISHES WHAT I DARE NOT TELL.'

'What would she have now?' asked the Fish.

'She wants to be Ruler of the Universe!' shouted the fisherman.

'Return, and find her back in her hovel of a hut,' said the Flounder, and disappeared.

And in that hut the fisherman and his wife remained for the remainder of their lives.

Impossible Judgement

Nobody can be sure whether any given tale originates with the written form and has from there passed into folklore: or the other way about. Some traditional tales are actually presented as true stories, even in modern biographies. Among these is this one, claimed to be an incident in the life of Lord Chancellor Egerton of England (died 1617) and also attributed to a case of Attorney-General William Noy (died 1634). Yet the same story is found in the writings of Valerius Maximus, nearly two thousand years ago! It is attributed to Demosthenes, who died in 322 BC, and reappears, according to a cardinal, as having actually happened in the Italian family of Lambertini in the 14th century. Here is a version taken from the novel by Le Sage, The History of Vanillo Gonzales, *supposedly from a Spanish original, published in 1734, two thousand years after its first attribution. Presumably the modern writers had not heard of the judgement scene in Shakespeare's* The Merchant of Venice.

THREE MERCHANTS, NAMED Charles Azarini, Peter Scannati and Jerom Avellino, went to the house of a venerable citizen of Palermo, Sicily, taking with them a notary public and ten thousand gold pieces. The old man agreed, in writing, to look after the money and not to give it up to any one of them unless in the presence of the two others. The agreement was duly notarised.

The money was carefully looked after until, some months later, Avellino knocked on the door during the night, most urgently, saying that the money was needed. Azarini, Scannati and he, he said, had an opportunity of buying a valuable cargo if they could move quickly.

'But you seem to forget that I cannot give you the money, according to our contract, unless all of you are present,' said the old man.

'I do indeed remember it,' said Avellino, 'but Azarini and Scannati are ill, and cannot come. But they are in agreement that you yield the money to me. Surely you remember that you have known me for a long time, and that I am an honest man?'

The old man was at first uncertain what he should do; but eventually he overcame his fears, and parted with the gold.

Avellino, of course, made off with the money, and thenceforward was nowhere to be found. No sooner did Azarini and Scannati hear what had happened than they brought a suit against the old man for the recovery of their money.

The case was heard by the Duke of Ossuna, Governor of Sicily, who, after the plaintiffs had been heard, asked the ancient, whose name was Giannetino, what answer he had to the charge.

'None whatever, Sir.'

Now the Duke said:

'He has no answer to make. He accepts that he owes you ten thousand crowns, and he is ready to do so. By the terms of the agreement, however, he can only pay you if and when all three of you are present together. Therefore bring Avellino into court, and the money shall be paid to you.'

Hudden and Dudden and Donald O'Neary

This Irish presentation of a very ancient tale, known for centuries among disparate peoples, was collected by Alfred Nutt in the nineteenth century, and it gives the literal narrative flavour of local phrase and emphasis, with no literary polishing. The theme is that of the trickster – Uncle Capriano in Sicily, Capdarmère in Gascony, Unibos in the eleventh-century Latin, Kibitz (Lapwing) in Germany – who profits from others' weaknesses. Incidents vary, but some are remarkably consistent in the various countries. The hero sells things to people whose avarice makes them believe that these things are, for instance, gold-giving hides. Hypocrites (like the priest who is a woman's illicit lover in certain variants) are trapped: 'magic' is performed by extra information concealed from the audience. The tale is found in the earliest European collection of popular tales, Straparola's published in Venice in 1550, and is reported from Africa, India and Scandinavia in numerous varieties. An

analysis of incidents may show something about the connections of the several versions, but it gives few clues as to how the diffusion may have come about. Some of this information is surprising: the Norse and Italian cognates are unusually close; so are the Icelandic and Indian versions – and the German and some Indian renderings. For some reason, the trickster's career is often initiated by some act of aggression of theft against him: before this event he seems to have been an ordinary, innocent, and law-abiding person. Commentators have been known to state that this fact proves that the story is a prefiguring of the theory that people may be forced into a life of crime or deception by the actions of others. Whether this delinquency, however occasioned, is likely to end, as these tales do, with the complete victory of the trickster, is another matter.

Once upon a time there were two farmers, and their names were Hudden and Dudden. They had poultry in their yards, sheep on the uplands, and scores of cattle in the meadow-land alongside the river. But for all that they were not happy. For just between their two farms there lived a poor man by the name of Donald O'Neary. He had a hovel over his head and a strip of grass that was barely enough to keep his one cow, Daisy, from starving; and, though she did her best, it was but seldom that Donald got a drink of milk or a roll of butter from Daisy. You would think that there was little here to make Hudden and Dudden jealous, but so it is, the more one has the more one wants, and Donald's neighbours lay awake of nights scheming how they might get hold of his little strip of grassland. Daisy, poor thing, they never thought of; she was just a bag of bones.

One day Hudden met Dudden, and they were soon grumbling as usual, and all to the tune of 'If only we could get that vagabond Donald O'Neary out of the country'.

'Let's kill Daisy,' said Hudden at last; 'if that doesn't make him clear out, nothing will.'

No sooner said than agreed, and it wasn't dark before Hudden and Dudden crept up to the little shed where lay poor Daisy trying her best to chew the cud, though she hadn't had as much grass in the day as would cover your hand. And when Donald came to see if Daisy was all snug for the night, the poor beast had only time to lick his hand once before she died.

Well, Donald was a shrewd fellow, and down-hearted though he was, began to think if he could get any good out of Daisy's death. He thought and he thought, and the next day you could have seen him trudging off early to the fair, Daisy's hide over his shoulder, every penny he had jingling in his pockets. Just before he got to the fair, he made several slits in the hide and put a penny in each slit. Then he walked into the best inn of the town as bold as if it belonged to him, and, hanging the hide up on a nail in the wall, sat down.

'Some of your best whiskey,' said he to the landlord. But the landlord didn't like his looks. 'Is it fearing I won't pay you, you are?' said Donald. 'Why I have a hide here that gives me all the money I want.' And with that he hit it a whack with his stick and out hopped a penny. The landlord opened his eyes, as you may fancy.

'What'll you take for that hide?'

'It's not for sale, my good man.'

'Will you take a gold piece?'

'It's not for sale I tell you. Hasn't it kept me and mine for years?' and with that Donald hit the hide another whack and out jumped a second penny.

Well, the long and short of it was that Donald let the hide go for a pile of gold; and, that very evening, who but he should walk up to Hudden's door?

'Good-evening, Hudden. Will you lend me your best pair of scales?'

Hudden stared and Hudden scratched his head, but he lent the scales.

When Donald was safe at home, he pulled out his pocketful of bright gold and began to weigh each piece in the scales. But Hudden had put a lump of butter at the bottom, and so the last piece of gold stuck fast to the scales when he took them back to Hudden.

If Hudden had stared before, he stared ten times more now, and no sooner was Donald's back turned, than he was off as hard as he could pelt to Dudden's.

'Good-evening, Dudden. That vagabond, bad luck to him…'

'You mean Donald O'Neary?'

'And who else should I mean? He's back here weighing out sackfuls of gold.'

'How do you know that?'

'Here are my scales that he borrowed, and here's a gold piece still sticking to them.'

Off they went together, and they came to Donald's door. Donald had finished making the last pile of ten gold pieces. And he couldn't finish because a piece had stuck to the scales.

In they walked without an 'If you please' or 'By your leave'.

'Well, I never!' was all they could say.

'Good-evening, Hudden, good-evening Dudden. Ah! you thought you had played me a fine trick, but you never did me a better turn in all your lives. When I found poor Daisy dead, I thought to myself, 'Well, her hide may fetch something", and it did. Hides are worth their weight in gold in the market just now.'

Hudden nudged Dudden, and Dudden winked at Hudden.

'Good-evening, Donald O'Neary.'

'Good-evening, kind friends.'

The next day there wasn't a cow or a calf that belonged to Hudden or Dudden but her hide was going to the fair in Hudden's biggest cart drawn by Dudden's strongest pair of horses.

When they came to the fair, each one took a hide over his arm, and there they were walking through the fair, bawling out at the top of their voices, 'Hides to sell! Hides to sell!'

Out came the tanner.

'How much for your hides, my good men?'

'Their weight in gold.'

'It's early in the day to come out of the tavern.' That was all the tanner said, and back he went to his yard.

'Hides to sell! Fine fresh hides to sell!'

Out came the cobbler.

'How much for your hides, my men?'

'Their weight in gold.'

'Is it making game of me you are! Take that for your pains,' and the cobbler dealt Hudden a blow that made him stagger.

Up the people came running from one end of the fair to the other. 'What's the matter? What's the matter?' cried they.

'Here are a couple of vagabonds selling hides at their weight in gold,' said the cobbler.

'Hold 'em fast, hold 'em fast!' bawled the innkeeper, who was the last to come up, he was so fat. 'I'll wager it's one of the rogues who tricked me out of thirty gold pieces yesterday for a wretched hide.'

It was more kicks than halfpence that Hudden and Dudden got before they were well on their way home again, and they didn't run the slower because all the dogs of the town were at their heels.

Well, as you may fancy, if they loved Donald little before, they loved him less now.

'What's the matter, friends?' said he as he saw them tearing along, their hats knocked in and their coats torn off and their faces black and blue. 'Is it fighting you've been? Or mayhap you met the police, ill luck to them?'

'We'll police you, you vagabond. It's mighty smart you thought yourself to be, deluding us with your lying tales.'

'Who deluded you? Didn't you see the gold with your own two eyes?'

But it was no use talking. Pay for it he must, and should. There was a meal-sack handy, and into it Hudden and Dudden popped Donald O'Neary, tied him up tight, ran a pole through the knot, and off they started for the Brown Lake of the Bog, each with a pole-end on his shoulder, and Donald O'Neary between.

But the Brown Lake was far, the road was dusty, Hudden and Dudden were sore and weary, and they were parched with thirst. There was an inn by the roadside.

'Let's go in,' said Hudden, 'I'm dead beat. It's heavy he is for the little he had to eat.'

If Hudden was willing, so was Dudden. As for Donald, you may be sure his leave wasn't asked, but he was dumped down at the inn door for all the world as if he had been a sack of potatoes.

'Sit still, you vagabond,' said Dudden, 'if we don't mind waiting, you needn't.'

Donald held his peace, but after a while he heard the glasses clink, and Hudden singing away at the top of his voice.

'I won't have her, I tell you; I won't have her!' said Donald. But nobody heeded what he said.

'I won't have her, I tell you; I won't have her!' said Donald, and this time he said it louder; but nobody heeded what he said.

'I won't have her, I tell you; I won't have her!' said

Donald; and this time he said it as loud as he could.

'And who won't you have may I be so bold as to ask?' said a farmer, who had just come up with a drove of cattle and was turning in for a glass.

'It's the King's daughter. They are bothering the life out of me to marry her.'

'You're the lucky fellow. I'd give something to be in your shoes.'

'Do you see that now! Wouldn't it be a fine thing for a farmer to be marrying a Princess, all dressed in gold and jewels?'

'Jewels, do you say? Ah, now, couldn't you take me with you?'

'Well, you're an honest fellow, and as I don't care for the King's daughter though she's as beautiful as the day, and is covered in jewels from top to toe, you shall have her. Just undo the cord, and let me out, they tied me up tight, as they knew I'd run away from her.'

Out crawled Donald, in crept the farmer.

'Now lie still, and don't mind the shaking, it's only rumbling over the palace steps you'll be. And maybe they'll abuse you for a vagabond, who won't have the King's daughter, but you needn't mind that. Ah! it's a deal I'm giving up for you, sure as it is that I don't care for the Princess.'

'Take my cattle in exchange,' said the farmer; and you may guess it wasn't long before Donald was at their tails driving them homewards.

Out came Hudden and Dudden, and the one took one end of the pole, and the other the other.

'I'm thinking he's heavier,' said Hudden.

'Ah, never mind,' said Dudden: 'it's only a step now to the Brown Lake.'

'I'll have her now! I'll have her now!' bawled the farmer, from inside the sack.

'By my faith, and you shall though,' said Hudden, and he laid his stick across the sack.

'I'll have her! I'll have her!' bawled the farmer louder than ever.

'Well, here you are,' said Dudden for they were now come to the Brown Lake, and, unslinging the sack, they pitched it plumb into the lake.

'You'll not be playing your tricks on us any longer,' said Hudden.

'True for you,' said Dudden. 'Ah, Donald, my boy, it was an ill day for you when you borrowed my scales.'

Off they went, with a light step and an easy heart, but when they were near home, who should they see but Donald O'Neary, and all around him the cows were grazing, and the calves were kicking up their heels and butting their heads together.

'Is it you, Donald?' said Dudden. 'Faith, you've been quicker than we have.'

'True for you, Dudden, and let me thank you kindly; the turn was good, if the will was ill. You'll have heard, like me, that the Brown Lake leads to the

Land of Promise. I always put it down as lies, but it is just as true as my word. Look at the cattle.'

Hudden stared, and Dudden gaped, but they couldn't get over the cattle, fine fat cattle they were too.

'It's only the worst I could bring up with me,' said Donald O'Neary, 'the others were so fat, there was no driving them. Faith, too, it's little wonder they didn't care to leave, with grass as far as you could see, and as sweet and juicy as fresh butter.'

'Ah, now Donald, we haven't always been friends,' said Dudden, 'but, as I was just saying, you were ever a decent lad, and you'll show us the way, won't you?'

'I don't see that I'm called upon to do that, there is a power more cattle down there. Why shouldn't I have them all to myself?'

'Faith, they may well say, the richer you get, the harder the heart. You always were a neighbourly lad, Donald. You wouldn't wish to keep all the luck to yourself?'

'True for you, Hudden, though 'tis a bad example you set me. But I'll not be thinking of old times. There is plenty for all there, so come along with me.'

Off they trudged, with a light heart and an eager step. When they came to Brown Lake, the sky was full of little white clouds, and, if the sky was full, the lake was just as full.

'Ah! now, look, there they are,' cried Donald, as he pointed to the clouds in the lake.

‘Where? Where?’ cried Hudden, and ‘Don’t be greedy!’ cried Dudden, as he jumped his hardest to be up first with the fat cattle. But if he jumped first, Hudden wasn’t long behind.

They never came back. Maybe they got too fat, like the cattle. As for Donald O’Neary, he had cattle and sheep all his days to his heart’s content.

Riquet with the Tuft

The earliest collection of popular tales in relatively modern times is the Piacevoli Notti *of Straparola, published in Venice in 1550 – some three thousand years after the Egyptians were recording some of their own legends. The book was banned in 1606 and placed on the Vatican Index, as two centuries later the Grimms' work was banned in Vienna for 'encouraging superstition'.*

Apart from often ignoring the question of a sound moral, the traditional story's 'superstitious' content may have included deeper implications. The Riquet tale, transmitted by Charles Perrault in the 18th century, could be taken as suggesting that humanity, within its often somewhat ugly outer husk, has a potential for transformation and inner beauty.

'Beauty and the Beast' has been characterised, for similar reasons, as a Buddhist-inspired tract, though the transformation or development theme is far from being a Buddhist monopoly.

'Riquet with the Tuft' is one of the first eight tales in the book which includes 'Sleeping Beauty', 'Little Red Riding-

Hood', 'Bluebeard', 'Puss-in-Boots' and 'Cinderella'. These 'Mother Goose's Tales', issued in 1697 and translated thirty-two years later into English, are thought to have hit the British Isles with such force as to knock out most of the ancient English stories, which thereafter became difficult to locate.

Written for the French Court and dedicated to the niece of King Louis XIV, the stories are certainly romanticised from what one would expect from the lips of country folk-reciters, but yet they have a far greater flavour of recitation than the stories of other collectors. Altogether, this specimen gives an excellent example of how Perrault handled his themes.

Once upon a time there was a Queen, who brought into the world a son so ugly and so ill-shaped that it was for a long time doubtful if he possessed a human form. A Fairy, who was present at his birth, affirmed that he would not fail to be amiable, as he would have much good sense. She added that he would be able, because of the gift with which she had endowed him, to impart equal intelligence to the person he should love best.

All this consoled the poor Queen a little, who was much distressed at having brought into the world so hideous a little monkey. It is true that the child was no sooner able to speak than he said a thousand pretty things, and that there was in all his actions an indescribable air of intelligence which charmed one.

I had forgotten to say that he was born with a little tuft of hair on his head, which caused him to be named Riquet with the Tuft, for Riquet was the family name.

At the end of seven or eight years, the Queen of a neighbouring kingdom gave birth to two daughters. The first that came into the world was fairer than day. The Queen was so delighted that it was feared her great joy would prove hurtful to her. The same Fairy who had assisted at the birth of little Riquet with the Tuft was present upon this occasion, and to moderate the joy of the Queen, she declared to her that this little Princess would have no mental capacity, and that she would be as stupid as she was beautiful.

This mortified the Queen exceedingly, but a few minutes afterwards she experienced a very much greater annoyance, for the second girl to which she gave birth proved to be extremely ugly. 'Do not distress yourself so much, Madam,' said the Fairy to her. 'Your daughter will find compensation; she will have so much sense that her lack of beauty will scarcely be perceived.'

'Heaven send it may be so,' replied the Queen; 'but are there no means of giving a little sense to the elder, who is so lovely?'

'I can do nothing for her, Madam, in the way of wit,' said the Fairy, 'but everything in that of beauty; and as there is nothing in my power that I would not do to gratify you, I will endow her with the ability to make beautiful the person who shall please her.'

As these two Princesses grew up, their endowments increased in the same proportion, and nothing was talked of anywhere but the beauty of the eldest and the intelligence of the youngest.

It is true that their defects also greatly increased with their years. The younger became uglier every instant, and the elder more stupid every day. She either made no answer when spoken to, or she said something foolish. With this she was so awkward, that she could not place four pieces of china on a mantelshelf without breaking one of them, nor drink a glass of water without spilling half of it on her dress.

Notwithstanding the great advantage of beauty to a girl, the younger bore away the palm from her sister nearly always in every society. At first they gathered round the handsomer to gaze at and admire her; but they soon left her for the wittier, to listen to a thousand agreeable things; and people were astonished to find that, in less than a quarter of an hour, the elder had not a soul near her, and that all the company had formed a circle round the younger. The former, though very stupid, noticed this, and would have given, without regret, all her beauty for half the sense of her sister.

The Queen, discreet as she was, could not help reproaching her frequently with her folly, which made the poor Princess ready to die of grief.

One day when she had withdrawn into a wood to bewail her misfortune, she saw a little man approach her, of most disagreeable appearance, but dressed very magnificently. It was the young Prince Riquet with the Tuft. He had fallen in love with her from seeing her portraits, which were sent all round the world, and had quitted his father's kingdom to have the pleasure of beholding her and speaking to her. Enchanted to meet her thus alone, he accosted her with all the respect and politeness imaginable.

Having remarked, after paying the usual compliments, that she was very melancholy, he said to her, 'I cannot comprehend, Madam, how a person so beautiful as you are can be so sad as you appear; for though I may boast of having seen an infinity of lovely women, I can say that I have never beheld one whose beauty could be compared to yours.'

'You are pleased to say so, Sir,' replied the Princess; and there she stopped.

'Beauty,' continued Riquet, 'is so great an advantage that it ought to surpass all others. When one possesses it as you do, I do not see anything that could very much distress you.'

'I would rather,' said the Princess, 'be as ugly as you, and have good sense, than possess the beauty I do, and be as stupid as I am.'

'There is no greater proof of good sense, Madam, than the belief that we have it not; it is the nature of that gift, that the more we have, the more we believe we are deficient of it.'

'I do not know how that may be,' said the Princess, 'but I know well enough that I am very stupid, and that is the cause of the grief which is killing me.'

'If that is all that afflicts you, Madam, I can easily put an end to your sorrow,' said Riquet.

'And how would you do that?' said the Princess.

'I have the power, Madam,' said Riquet with the Tuft, 'to give as much wit as any one can possess to the person I love the most; and as you, Madam, are that person, it will depend entirely upon yourself whether or not you will have so much wit, provided that you are willing to marry me.'

The Princess was thunderstruck, and replied not a word.

'I see,' said Riquet with the Tuft, 'that this proposal pains you; and I am not surprised at it; but I give you a full year to consider it.'

The Princess had so little sense, and at the same time was so anxious to have a great deal, that she thought the end of the year would never come; so she accepted at once the offer that was made her.

She had no sooner promised Riquet with the Tuft that she would marry him that day twelve months ahead than she felt herself to be quite another person from what she was previously. She found she possessed an incredible facility of saying anything she wished, and of saying it in a shrewd, yet easy and natural manner.

She commenced on the instant, and kept up a sprightly conversation with Riquet with the Tuft, during which she chatted away at such a rate, that Riquet with the Tuft began to believe he had given her more wit than he had kept for himself.

When she returned to the palace, the whole court was puzzled to account for a change so sudden and extraordinary, for in proportion to the number of foolish things they had heard her say formerly, were the sensible and exceedingly clever observations to which she now gave utterance.

All the court was in a state of joy which is not to be conceived. The younger sister alone was not very much pleased. No longer possessing over her elder sister the advantage of wit, she now only appeared, by her side, as a very disagreeable-looking person. The King was now led by his elder daughter's advice, and sometimes even held his council in her apartment.

The news of this alteration having spread abroad, all the young Princes of the neighbouring kingdoms exerted themselves to obtain her affection, and nearly all of them asked her hand in marriage; but she found none of them sufficiently intelligent, and she listened to all of them without engaging herself to any one.

At length arrived a Prince so rich, so witty and so handsome that she could not help feeling an inclination for him. Her father, having perceived it, told her that he left her at perfect liberty to choose a husband for herself, and that she had only to make known her decision.

As the more sense we possess, the more difficulty we find in making up the mind positively on such a matter, she requested, after having thanked her father, that he would allow her some time to think of it.

She went, by chance, to walk in the same wood where she had met with Riquet with the Tuft, in order to ponder with greater freedom on what she had to do. While she was walking deep in thought, she heard a dull sound beneath her feet, as of many persons running to and fro, and busily occupied.

Having listened more attentively, she heard one say, 'Bring me that saucepan,' another, 'Give me that kettle,' another, 'Put some wood on the fire.'

At the same moment the ground opened, and she saw beneath her, what appeared to be a large kitchen, full of cooks, scullions and all sorts of servants necessary for the preparation of a magnificent banquet. There came forth a band of from twenty to thirty cooks, who went and established themselves in an avenue of the wood at a very long table, and who, each with a larding-pin in hand, set to work, keeping time to a melodious song.

The Princess, astonished at this sight, enquired for whom they were working.

'Madam,' replied the most prominent of the troop, 'for Prince Riquet with the Tuft, whose marriage will take place tomorrow.'

The Princess, still more surprised than she was before, and suddenly recollecting that it was just a twelvemonth from the day on which she had promised to marry Prince Riquet with the Tuft, was lost in amazement. The cause of her not having remembered her promise was, that when she made it she was a fool, and on receiving her new mind, she forgot all her follies.

She had not taken thirty steps in continuation of her walk, when Riquet with the Tuft presented himself before her, gaily and magnificently attired, like a Prince about to be married.

'You see, Madam,' said he, 'I have kept my word punctually, and I doubt not but that you have come hither to keep yours, and to make me, by the gift of your hand, the happiest of men.'

'I confess to you frankly,' replied the Princess, 'that I have not yet made up my mind on that matter, and that I do not think I shall ever be able to do so to your satisfaction.'

'You astonish me, Madam,' said Riquet with the Tuft.

'I have no doubt I do,' said the Princess; 'and assuredly, had I to deal with a stupid person – a man without mind – I should feel greatly embarrassed. "A Princess is bound by her word," he would say to me, "and you must marry me, as you have promised to do so." But as the person to whom I speak is the most sensible man in all the world, I am certain he will listen to reason. You know that, when I was no better than a fool, I nevertheless could not resolve to marry you – how can you expect, now that I have the sense which you have given me, and which renders me much more difficult to please than before, that I should take a decision today which I could not do then. If you seriously thought of marrying me, you did very wrongly to take away my stupidity, and enable me to see more clearly than I saw then.'

'If a man without sense,' replied Riquet with the Tuft, 'should meet with some indulgence, as you have just intimated, were he to reproach you with your breach of promise, why would you expect, Madam, that I should not be equally so in a matter which affects the entire happiness of my life? Is it reasonable that persons of intellect should be in a worse condition than those that have none? Can you assert this – you who have so much and have so earnestly desired to possess it? But let us come to the point, if you please. With the exception of my ugliness, is there anything in me that displeases you? Are you dissatisfied with my birth, my understanding, my temper or my manners?'

'Not in the least,' replied the Princess; 'I admire in you everything you have mentioned.'

'If so,' rejoined Riquet with the Tuft, 'I shall be happy, as you have it in your power to make me the most agreeable of men.'

'How can that be done?' said the Princess.

'It can be done,' said Riquet with the Tuft, 'if you love me sufficiently to wish that it should be. And in order, Madam, that you should have no doubt about it, know that the same fairy who, on the day I was born, endowed me with the power to give understanding to the person I chose, gave you also the power to render handsome the man you should love, and on whom you wished to bestow that favour.'

'If such be the fact,' said the Princess, 'I wish, with

all my heart, that you should become the handsomest Prince in the world, and I bestow the gift on you to the fullest extent in my power.'

The Princess had no sooner pronounced these words than Riquet with the Tuft appeared to her eyes, of all men in the world, the handsomest, the best made, and most amiable she had ever seen.

There are some who assert that it was not the spell of the Fairy, but love alone that caused this metamorphosis. They say that the Princess, having reflected on the perseverance of her lover – on his prudence, and all the good qualities of his heart and mind – no longer saw the deformity of his body nor the ugliness of his features, that his hunch appeared to her nothing more than the effect of a man shrugging his shoulders, and that instead of observing, as she had done, that he limped horribly, she saw in him no more than a certain lounging air, which charmed her.

They say also that his eyes, which squinted, seemed to her only more brilliant from that defect, which passed in her mind from a proof of the intensity of his love, and, in fine that his great red nose had in it something martial. However this may be, the Princess promised on the spot to marry him, provided he obtained the consent of the King, her father.

The King having learned that his daughter entertained a great regard for Riquet with the Tuft, whom he knew also to be a very clever and wise